The Evolution of A Leader

by

Terry Weaver

BROTHER,
THANK YOU MOST
OF ALL FOR YOUR
HEART TO SERVES OTHERS.
THAT IS WHAT SETS US APART.
HERE IS TO OUR EVOLUTION AS
LEADERS.

YOUR BROTHER,
TOMMY DENVER
6/14/19

PRAISE FOR THE EVOLUTION OF A LEADER

"In *The Evolution of A Leader,* Terry Weaver captured the essence of leadership development. Looking back over a forty-one-year career in the Marine Corps, retiring as a Lieutenant General, I wish that I would have possessed and read this book when I was a sergeant in the Marine Corps at the beginning of a career of leadership. Read and refer to this book over and over as a developing leader, then do great things."
– Steven Hummer, Lieutenant General, United States Marine Corps (Ret.)

"I read with great connection Terry's book *The Evolution of a Leader.* As a student of leadership, someone who is pursuing a Ph.D. in Executive Leadership and someone who has mentored and led literally hundreds of leaders in successful teams, I was captivated by Terry's book. He brings to light the growth path of a Leader and how the path develops a Leader's Influence and Impact. His ability to connect real-life examples with proven leadership principles is uncanny. His use of historically recognized leaders in industry, life, and education bring the evolutionary path full circle back to the individual. It is this ability that makes this book relevant, influential and a must read for anyone working to create their path of leading and influencing others to Impact. I plan to give this book to many of my mentee's and clients and also use it as a source for my teachings."
– Bob Milner / Serial Entrepreneur, Professor of Entrepreneurship & Leadership

"Terry's book will inspire you! It is a guide, with markers, for you to grow as a leader and serve others well. You will want to keep it as a reference."
– Bob Koenig - Leader, Entrepreneur & Founder of Andrew Coaching, LLC

"This inspiring book is for anyone wanting to build a life of a career that will stand the test of time. It's packed full of practical wisdom to assist you on becoming the leader you were born to be."
– Thomas Gordon Polonys, Educator & Author of Life or Death.

"*The Evolution of A Leader* is one of the best tools anyone can use to sharpen their minds and souls. It is more than a book; this is a collection of brilliant stories, remarkable examples and a ton of actionable steps. This is a must read for all aspiring leaders."
– Josh Cherry, CEO & Director of Franchising Delta Life Franchising, LLC

"Terry's articulations on leadership are spot on in his new book *The Evolution of A Leader*. This book is a must read."
– Gordy Bunch, Founder & CEO of TWFG, Ernst & Young Entrepreneur of the Year and U.S. Coast Guard Veteran

"Continual growth is a must in life and especially in leadership. I love how *The Evolution of A Leader* knits together key learnings from great leaders as well as new ideas into a well written thoughtful book. Mr. Weaver's anecdotes are not only personal but relatable. Well done!"
– Debra Myers, Founder & CEO Enfusia & Muscle Rehab

DEDICATION

This book is dedicated to my wife Chelley, my children Laura, Zen, Presley, Liam, and my Heavenly Father.

Thanks for inspiring me to be the man I am today.

TABLE OF CONTENTS

1. Your Evolution

"I built my talents on the shoulders of someone else's talent. I believe greatness is an evolutionary process that changes and evolves era to era."

Michael Jordan[1]

What does it take to become a leader?

What or who is a leader?

Is a leader merely someone out front, or is being a leader much more?

Are leaders born or made?

Are leaders some combination of genetic chance and life experience?

How do you start the lifelong pursuit of leading....today?

These are all questions that I have asked myself throughout my personal leadership journey. I've had to look for examples and search history for a conclusion to these questions. My findings are laid out in this book.

It took me twenty years of research and life experience to produce this book. It can be used as reference no matter what stage of the leadership journey you are on.

At the start of this writing my theory was that leadership is an evolutionary process... It is a journey that great leaders never desire to complete. Great leaders continue their evolution, so they can become more effective at leading others. The first warning sign of a leader's decline is when they conclude that they have completed their leadership development and they have nothing left to learn.

This book is meant to be a manual for you to use and refer back to often. The evolution of a leader is an ongoing process that requires constant attention. We should wake up daily expecting to continue our personal mission of becoming a more impactful leader. It should excite us that our leadership journey is never ending and that every day is an opportunity to write a new line into our leadership story.

My hope is that this book will encourage you to view your life and the significant opportunity that lies ahead of you as a never-ending quest to continue your personal leadership development. Your personal leadership journey can lead to massive impact, or little to nothing depending on the way you view it and act upon it.

Leaders make an impact in life. They change the way people think and act, and great leaders see their leadership journey as a calling rather than a position or a role. They understand the responsibility that comes with leadership. Good leaders understand they have a limited amount of time to leave a legacy and do the work they were created for.

This book will expose to you leadership principles that are timeless. These principles are just as effective today as they were 200 years ago. The principles that are outlined here will never fade or become extinct. In fact, the principles discussed in this book were demonstrated by some of the greatest leaders of history such as: Abraham Lincoln, Theodore Roosevelt, Andrew Carnegie, Socrates, Albert Einstein, King David, and Jesus Christ. They are also principles that are discussed and used by contemporary leaders such as John Maxwell, Brené Brown, Carol Dweck, Tony Robbins and many others who have influenced this text.

Hopefully you will quickly realize that leadership is a way of life. It is an "*operating system*" that is built upon principles and values. If you understand the principles and values, you can become the very best version of yourself. You will realize that there is no better time to start or continue your leadership journey than **today**. In fact, there is no perfect time. There is only the present time, and the present is the only time ripe and primed for action, so my encouragement for you is to embrace *The Evolution of A Leader* today.

2. Begin Today

*"Life shrinks or expands
in proportion to one's courage."*
Anais Nin[2]

Leaders are unique – they stand out. It takes courage to step out of the herd and do something unlike everyone else. It takes courage to be a leader, and it is not for the faint of heart. Not only does it take courage to lead, but it also takes being comfortable with showing ourselves – our true selves.

Many people will never step out of the herd because of the fear of the unknown and of being different. Leaders have to deal with and overcome one of the hardest questions that all of humanity wrestles with – *"what will others think of me if I do this*?" It does not matter what you are thinking about doing, the fear is real. It is a haunting feeling; so haunting that it holds most people back from pursuing their dreams and goals.

To be able to lead, and do something significant, leaders must deal with their fear of the unknown. As leaders, we have to be okay with two things: **not knowing** and sometimes **not caring** what others will think or say when we act on what we believe we are being called to do.

Leaders have to be able to make a declaration to the universe that they are moving forward in courage despite what may happen.

So right now, before you read any further, I challenge you to make your declaration to the universe stating what you intend to do. This could be a dream that you have had to start a business, finish a degree, pursue a passion or stop a bad habit. You can say this in many ways, but I suggest starting by exclaiming, HEY UNIVERSE, I AM GOING TO......!

Declare it here:

_____

_____

_____

_____

_____

This is not a one-time occurrence. You will have to declare this often because the critics are pervasive. It is also helpful to place your declaration on your bathroom mirror so you can see it and repeat it to yourself daily. Not only are there external critics, but there are also critics we fight in our own minds. External and internal critics use the same tactics: doubt, insecurity, fear and shame. We can identify these critics and stop them before they get a foothold – this book will help equip you to do that.

When one steps out to lead...count on it, there will be naysayers and critics. Theodore Roosevelt, the 26th President of The United States of America, wrote one of the most eloquent statements about being courageous and stepping into the arena,

The Man in the Arena[3]

"It is not the critic who counts; not the man who points out how the strong man stumbles, or where the doer of deeds could have done them better. The credit belongs to the man who is actually in the arena, whose face is marred by dust and sweat and blood; who strives valiantly; who errs, who comes short again and again, because there is no effort without error and shortcoming; but who does actually strive to do the deeds; who knows great enthusiasms, the great devotions; who spends himself in a worthy cause; who at the best knows in the end the triumph of high achievement, and who at the worst, if he fails, at least fails while daring greatly, so that his place

shall never be with those cold and timid souls who

neither know victory nor defeat."

The **arena** for us as leaders is the point in time that we step out into the unknown. All kinds of critics will appear, but we must remember as Roosevelt said, "*It is not the critic who counts….the credit belongs to the man who is actually in the arena.*" The only requirement to become a critic is insecurity. The buy in for the critic is very low, and they always stand far from the actual arena. I encourage you to refer back to *The Man in the Arena* if and when you begin to doubt your journey.

Because leaders are out front, it is true that it can become very lonely. It can sometimes feel like we are living on an island isolated from all others. This leads us to a very important truth that we would be wise to embrace...the idea that – ***true strength comes from the courage to ask for help.***

Can we lead in the absence of good relationships? The answer is "*No.*" Everyone needs help sometimes, and since we were put on this Earth to be in relationship with others, the worst thing we can do is attempt to live life and do leadership alone. When we make the decision to ask for help, endless possibilities open themselves to us because we choose to leave isolation, enter collaboration, and lead interdependently. Individual leaders begin the journey to become great leaders when they embrace the idea of needing and relying on help from others. One of the greatest leadership quotes I have ever found simply states, *"He who thinks he is leading and turns around to see no followers, is just taking a walk."*[4]

Leadership exists on the foundation of strong relationships. The strength of our relationships and their interdependence will determine our ability to lead.

- Relationships are the most important factor to our evolution as a leader.
- The second most important factor is our willingness to ask for help.

Henry Cloud reminds us,

> *"the undeniable reality is that how well you do in life and in business depends not only on what you do and how you do it, your skills and competencies, but also on who is doing it with you or to you. Who is helping you? Who is fighting you? Who is strengthening you or resisting and diminishing you? These people are literally making you who you are."*[5]

So, who are you as a leader?

Are you asking for help or trying to lead in some form of isolation?

Are you surrounded by leaders who can help you build the right foundation?

Are you evolving as a leader, or are you simply taking a walk?

3. Leaders and Imposters

"The thing that is really hard, and really amazing, is giving up on being perfect and beginning the work of becoming yourself"
Anna Quindlen[6]

What am I doing here?

Am I qualified for this?

I hope they don't find out who I really am!

When we decide to step out and lead, a flood of negative emotions and thoughts can begin to attack us.

In Steven Pressfield's masterpiece, *"The War of Art,"*[7] he calls the voice in our head that tries to stop us from our destiny – *"resistance."*

There is a common psychological phenomenon that has been studied and documented named the "Imposter Syndrome." This thought process is often associated with one's chosen occupation, educational achievement or career advancement. "Imposter Syndrome" is prevalent with over-achievers and those who have perfectionistic tendencies. However, it is not limited to these types of individuals.

There have been many studies on the "Imposter Syndrome" / Phenomenon, but early research performed by psychologists Dr. Suzanne Imes, PhD, and Dr. Pauline Rose Clance, PhD, in the 1970s explains, "*The impostor phenomenon occurs among high achievers who are unable to internalize and accept their success. They often attribute their accomplishments to luck rather than to ability and fear that others will eventually unmask them as a fraud.*"[8]

Since that original work, there have been numerous follow-up studies that confirm this is a human condition that is not limited to a specific race, sex or economic class.

Kirsten Weir explains in her summary of the imposter phenomenon, "*The impostor phenomenon seems to be more common among people who are embarking on a new endeavor….*"[9]

All leaders who step out and aspire to live significantly at some point in time are confronted with the thought of being an imposter. They often question if they are worthy of leading others. These doubts stem from many things including our life experiences and our own levels of self-worth. At some point successful leaders must recognize they can overcome the imposter phenomenon by believing they are called to something greater than self.

When we are called to something greater than self, our work is no longer about us…. It is about doing everything we can do to prepare for and accomplish our calling so we can serve others and answer our call.

We as leaders need to ask ourselves, *"If we don't step up and fulfill the call to lead, who will?"*

Our fundamental qualification for leading, is our own willingness to put ourselves up against a challenge and to right a wrong. If we decide to succumb to the idea that we may be an imposter, we will essentially deny our responsibility to engage in making our world a better place – we deny our calling.

Dr. Viktor Frankl, Psychiatrist and Holocaust survivor, received 29 honorary doctorates for his work in psychology. In his landmark book, *A Man's Search for Meaning*[10], he explains that we all must decide our own answer to the call of life. *"Ultimately, man should not ask what the meaning of his life is, but rather must recognize that it is he who is asked. In a word, each man is questioned by life; and he can only answer to life by answering for his own life; to life he can only respond by being responsible."*[11]

As leaders, we must believe in and accept our opportunity and responsibility to create a better world for everyone to live in. This life that each of us lives is calling out for greatness, for uniqueness, for a response to the great question – *"What will you do with this gift of life you have been given?"*

We get to choose the answer to this question that is asked of us. We get to choose to become the leaders that this world desperately needs. All leaders must identify their unique talents by accessing their dynamic minds and activating their unique potential.

There can never be even the smallest trace of imposter in us if we make the decision to define ourselves. There is no substitute for our unique and authentic self, for each of us is talented like no other. We must realize that our identity is not determined by our profession, our skills, our experience or the lack thereof. We were not designed to fit into a mold – we were designed to continue to break the molds that this world tries limit us with. Our identity can never be at risk if we know who we are and believe in our own unique design.

We must view our life as a vessel that we get to fill with whatever we choose. The things we pour into our life will eventually manifest as physical, psychological and emotional realities. When we think of our life as a vessel, we can imagine filling a pitcher with fluid; as we continue to pour into our pitcher of life, things will eventually spill over and flow out of our life. We must be careful and intentional about what we are pouring into our life. We are responsible for our vessel and what flows out of it. Our evolution as a leader continues as we pour the right ingredients into our life.

Lastly, leaders reject the idea of being an imposter by realizing that we as leaders, have been created to live a life of abundance.

The very building blocks of our biology – our cells, teach us that multiplication is a fundamental truth about who we are. Since we are designed to multiply, our lives should reflect growth. Since our nature is abundant in design, we can be confident that we are meant to grow and progress through life. By design we were meant to flourish, thrive and learn.

Because you are unique in your design and have the ability to learn, create and multiply – **the only decision left to make, is how you will answer the call this life is asking.**

4. Leaders and Creators

"The leader who accomplishes great things will not always be the most talented or the best educated –it will be the leader who refuses to put brackets on his thinking. It will be the leader who refuses to limit himself by what others have done or failed to do."

Andy Stanley[12]

In 2017 I heard Fredrik Haren say, *"When we are creating, we are most like God."*[13]

Whether that is true or not, the statement piqued my curiosity and I am better because of it. I began to wonder if I was creative, and if not, I asked *myself, "Could I become a creator?"*

I quickly realized that we all hold the ability to create, and that when we tap into our creativity; we come alive.

Some of the greatest potential inventions will stay trapped in the minds of their creators because of fear. They will be imagined then forgotten, and they will never benefit those who they were intended for.

All great creative breakthroughs are created twice...once in the mind of their inventors and once in reality when their inventor is bold enough to act on the idea they were inspired with.

Leaders are some of the greatest creators on this Earth. Leaders make a way where there was no way before them; they create opportunities for others. They help create relationships and businesses. They birth new ideas and bring them life. If you study leaders throughout time, you will notice just how innovative and creative they are. Leaders constantly step into the unknown to build things, reinvent things, or change things drastically through what is often referred to as *"Creative Destruction."*[1]

Oftentimes leaders lack appreciation for and underestimate the importance of creativity. Leaders fail to realize that creativity can be the innovative fuel that takes a team to new heights. A creative leader can be a catalyst for change, change that sets an entire organization ahead of the competition. To prove out this idea, let's take inventory of

---

[1] This term refers to the replacement of the old technology with the new. For example, fuel injectors replaced carburetors on cars because they were more fuel efficient but it unemployed people who made them. Similarly, digital media replaced vinyl records and those who pressed them. The term was first used in 1942 by the economist Joseph Schumpter. See "Capitalism, Socialism and Democracy," Harper & Brothers, 1947. 2nd edition

some of the most successful and creative companies of our time.

Apple®, Google®, Amazon®, and Samsung® are all Fortune 100® companies. But they also share another common theme within their business makeup. That theme is that the leaders of these companies hold that creativity is essential to their success. Creativity and innovation are the core strengths that have taken these companies from the garages, grocery stores, and college campuses they were started in, and have placed their products in almost every household across the globe. How is a creative company built? It starts with a leader who values creativity enough to develop a culture that embraces it.

Benjamin Franklin is one of my favorite creatives of the past. He was a leader, innovator, and self-taught scientist who consistently challenged the status quo. He helped create newspapers, eyeglasses, maps, new governments, moral codes, and success formulas. He helped organize peace treaties with the very nation he fought hard to liberate himself from, so how did he do it?

Franklin was intentional about not limiting his thinking. He set aside personal thinking time so that he could harness the power of his creativity. This led him to become a consummate creator many times over. He left a mark on history because he challenged himself to travel beyond the brackets of conventional thinking. He pushed boundaries and constantly questioned authority, and in turn, he created new standards instead of living in the norm.

Leaders are by definition out in the front. They are setting a course and showing others the way, and this alone takes creativity. Leaders need no cutting-edge equipment or education to challenge traditional thinking and create new ways to do things. To think and act creatively, one only needs the right mindset. A creative mindset is one without boundaries – one that explores uncharted territory.

One of the greatest examples of a leader who maintains a limitless creative mindset is Elon Musk. So far, Elon has disrupted at least four deeply entrenched industries: finance, transportation, energy, and space. These industries are old, competitive, and heavily regulated; at least they were before Elon creatively disrupted them. Now each of the industries have become new frontiers of innovation, and competition that Elon and his companies are dominating.

Creative minds see through problems to recognize opportunities.

Elon did not let the complexity or the competitive landscape stop him from innovating in these industries. He saw problems and instead of looking at the massive barriers to entry, he decided to see through them and expose the even larger opportunities.

Elon was born in 1971 in South Africa[14]. He tells stories of gazing at the stars as a child and thinking about the possibilities that would soon become a part his legacy. He likely looked to other creative forces and asked the question, *"Why are we not making progress in these arenas?"*

A little more than 100 years Elon's senior stood Henry Ford, one of the great innovators of the 19th century. He is best known for proliferating automobile manufacturing in the United States. One of Ford's most inspiring sayings that he used to challenge himself and others with is still repeated often by the creative minds of today.

> *"Whether you think you can or you think you cannot, you are right."*
> Henry Ford[15]

For close to 100 years the traditional automobile industry went relatively unchallenged.

Elon Musk took advantage of this with his creative mindset and literally reinvented the automobile. Elon asked himself, *"Why are we not building electric cars?"*

He asked the question, *"Why has the automobile industry used the same combustion engine for 100+ years?"*

He also asked other questions like, *"Why are we not harnessing the sun to power our world? Why are we not working on becoming a multi-planet people?"*

He believed he could disrupt the transportation, space and energy industries, and because of his creative mindset, he did it. Elon learned from his predecessor Henry Ford but did not follow his tradition. Instead, he stepped out to lead in a different direction. This is the way leaders create and use innovation to chart new paths.

Benjamin Franklin, Elon Musk and Henry Ford are examples of great creators who led our nation into better eras because they were not afraid to challenge people and ideas.

But first, they had to be bold enough to create something different, and if we want to be world-changing leaders, we must be unafraid to do the same thing.

We must have a creative mindset that looks at the current state of our country, people and businesses and pose the question, *"Why are we still doing it this way?"*

We must also remember, *"Whether we think we can or we think we cannot, we are right."*[16]

5. Leaders, Boundaries & Vision

"Finite players play within boundaries; infinite players play with boundaries."
James P. Carse[17]

It is true that we are physically bound by time and space, but even so, as leaders our vision of the future should be boundless.

Leaders are different because they see into the future using their minds' eye. They see things not as they are, but as they could be.

Leaders become great when they harness their limitless imagination and dream in color, paint outside the lines, and explore visions of what will take themselves and others into the future.

Let me give you an example of boundless.

> *It is true that as this book, The Evolution of A Leader, is being birthed out of my experience, ideas, and the*

history of great leaders, I am bound by time and space.

Or am I?

As visionaries and boundless thinkers, we should question and challenge traditional ideas. In fact it is true that I am writing today while transferring ideas, techniques and new ways of thinking to you in the future through time and space.

Stay with me for a minute!

I am typing these words now, November 26th, 2018, but I am also transferring these ideas through time to you at your current state.

Go with me one level deeper now.

*On November 23rd, I made a decision to write this book. I proclaimed to the universe, "**Hey universe, I am going to write a book and it is going to help a lot of people**".*

That decision changed the future.

It impacted me today because I sit here today challenging myself to help others through sharing powerful ideas.

And it impacted you at a future time; this book is meeting you where you are today, whenever that is. The book is showing you the power of visionary leadership, "*today.*"

This is a powerful idea, and if you can adopt this type of thinking, you will rid yourself of boundaries and become a visionary thinker.

"The best way to predict your future is to create it."
Peter Drucker[18]

Leaders believe they have an opportunity to make an impact in the lives of others through a vision that is much bigger than themselves.

Leaders understand the power of vision for themselves and for those they share it with. They understand that more than anything else, their thinking determines their future and the future of those they can influence. Leaders understand that thinking big or small is a self-fulfilling prophecy.

When leaders begin to believe that their ideas hold power to unlock potential and impact lives, everything changes.

Their thoughts become actions.

Their actions create progress.

That progress changes the world.

Progress changes the way we think, the way we act and the way we live. When leaders take action and make their ideas come to life, they begin to cause a ripple in the sea of mediocrity.

Remember this statement – *everything breaks down, yesterday's innovation is today's ordinary way of doing* business. This world needs leaders to constantly reinvent the way we think. Leaders understand that when they begin to share a vision with others, it challenges their thinking and could change the trajectory of their lives. This is a powerful truth, and it should be handled with responsibly.

> *I remember a time when I went and spoke on the topic of* **Our Ability to Change the Lives of Others Forever**. *I shared with the audience that each of us have gifts that we were meant to share with others and that these gifts were never meant to be held on to. If we decide not to share our gifts with the world, they lose their power.*
>
> *A few days after the talk I received a text message from an unknown number. It read, "Thanks for being a leader. You will never know just how many people you inspire. Thank u is not enough."*
>
> *My first thought was, I need to know who this is, but on second thought, I decided just to respond with a message of thanks!*

The unbound thinking and vision that leaders believe and communicate can accomplish seemingly impossible feats. At the height of the Cold War, President Kennedy saw a vision of what could be instead of the limitations of time and space. In 1962, in Houston Texas, Kennedy gave his awe inspiring speech about what America was capable of and what they would do:

"We choose to go to the moon in this decade and do the other things, not because they are easy, but because they are hard, because that goal will serve to organize and measure the best of our energies and skills, because that challenge is one that we are willing to accept, one we are unwilling to postpone, and one which we intend to win, and the others, too....

But if I were to say, my fellow citizens, that we shall send to the moon, 240,000 miles away from the control station in Houston, a giant rocket more than 300 feet tall, the length of this football field, made of new metal alloys, some of which have not yet been invented, capable of standing heat and stresses several times more than have ever been experienced, fitted together with a precision better than the finest watch, carrying all the equipment needed for propulsion, guidance, control, communications, food and survival, on an untried mission, to an unknown celestial body, and then return it safely to earth, re-entering the atmosphere at speeds of over 25,000 miles per hour, causing heat about half that of the temperature of the sun – almost as hot as it is here today – and do all this, and do it right, and do it first before this decade is out – then we must be bold...."

Well, space is there, and we're going to climb it, and the moon and the planets are there, and new hopes for knowledge and peace are there. And, therefore, as we set sail we ask God's blessing on

the most hazardous and dangerous and greatest
adventure on which man has ever embarked."[19]

Kennedy's speech caused a paradigm shift in what was
thought to be impossible, and it created a global and
arguably an interplanetary ripple effect in time and space.
Almost seven years later, the famous words, "*One giant leap
for mankind,*"[20] were heard and over a half-billion people
watched Neil Armstrong take his first moon walk. This is the
power of visionary leadership and boundless thinking.

Leaders realize that their vision must be big to inspire others
and lift them to a new level of thinking. We will never know
our impact – whether it is big or small, until we take action to
make it.

A text message of thanks or an outpouring of praise could
be all it takes to inspire another. Leaders believe that one
person changed is enough to realize that they have helped
elevate the precious spirit and mind of a priceless human
being. Leaders understand the power of vision and
boundless thinking.

6. Leaders are Learners

"An investment in knowledge pays the best interest."
Benjamin Franklin[21]

Our "operating system" as a leader is determined by our knowledge and wisdom. **Wisdom is knowledge in action.**

Wisdom is the very action of what we know, and the only way to increase our knowledge and wisdom is through continued learning. We can learn from many sources including experience, but we can also learn from traditional and non-traditional education, mentors, reading and the act of leading. We must never underestimate the power of knowledge, and we must maintain the position of being a lifelong student. Leaders who place a low emphasis on continuing to learn become features of "*Yesterday's Headlines.*" They become irrelevant because of the speed and proliferation of today's omnipresent information.

There's a story about a lumberjack contest that two men entered.

"The goal of the contest was to determine which man could chop down their respective tree the fastest. At the sound of the starting bell both men raced toward their axes and prepared themselves to chop down the equally sized trees. One of the men grabbed the axe and began to hack away at the base of the tree. But the other man did something that astonished not only his competitor but also the spectators. He grabbed hold of his axe, sat down on a nearby stump and began to sharpen the blade of his axe.

After a half hour of sharpening, he also began hacking at the base of his tree. The lumberjack who took time to sharpen his tool made significantly more progress that the lumberjack who settled for the tool that he was given.

Can you imagine how the story ends? The man who sat and took time to sharpen his blade won the contest and set a record time in doing it."[22]

You might be wondering what the point of this story is…..**we need to pay time and attention to the condition of our tools.** Leaders need to sharpen their tools often – maybe as often as they use them.

The great educator and learner Stephen Covey puts it this way, *"This is the single most powerful investment we can ever make in life – an investment in ourselves, in the only instrument we have with which to deal with life and to contribute."*[23]

I love this idea because it puts emphasis on one of the greatest inputs that a leader can have, and that is the input of knowledge. It is important to understand that we can have the heart to lead, we can have the best intentions, and we can have the drive to make things happen, but if we lack the knowledge and experience to lead, the other components may become useless. We cannot give away what we don't have, so we must remember to put a precedence on developing ourselves first so that we can pass on our knowledge to others. Covey and the story of the lumberjacks remind us that before we go to work leading, we must first sharpen ourselves and hone our abilities.

One of the best ways we can begin to invest in ourselves is by finding the giants who have gone before us and learning from them. In almost every industry, even emerging industries, there are giants – sometimes they are innovators or first movers who have set a standard that we can look to for guidance. Once we find these giants we can learn from them in a few different ways.

We can learn from their resources, and we can ask them for help directly through mentorship or some other way.

Leaders should never be afraid to reach out to a professional who has been achieving at the highest level for decades. It is likely that they asked for help when they were just beginning, and if they remember that, they may just agree to pay that help forward to you.

It is true that none are successful alone.

- The best-selling author needs the army of eager learners to purchase books.

- The recording artist needs the throng of fans to attend the concert.

- The NBA star basketball player needs the coaches through his lifetime, plus the fellow teammates and the builders of the arena who all help make him the star he is.

Most of these giants, at some point in their life, get to a place where they want to give back and help the fledgling leader. If you are proactive about asking for help, you may get to be their pupil.

Asking for help takes few things: it requires us to have the humility to say "*I need help,*" and the self-worth to believe "*I am worth helping.*" Both of these are true for you and me.

Remember – success is never created in a vacuum or isolation. Instead, success always requires collaboration! If leaders will embrace this idea, it will catapult them years ahead of those who buy into the lie…that they can do something significant all on their own without help.

Let me provide some practical examples.

> *When I decided to write this book, I also made a decision to collaborate with the giants of writing. I*

reached out for help from Stephen King, Steven Pressfield, Strunk & White, and many others. Before ever putting one word on a page, my creative journey began by assembling my team of giants. My team included great writers of the past and present who helped me along my creative process and joined me....not technically, but follow me for a moment. Before attempting to write this book I researched the writers who I thought could be a reference and mentor to me.

I went out and purchased Stephen King's book *"On Writing, A Memoir of the Craft"*[24] which is one part memoir and the other part writer's guide. This book gave me the framework and inspiration to start, and starting is half the battle. It also taught me much about Stephen's psychology of process.

I also purchased the audio book, *"The War of Art,"* by Steven Pressfield[25], and it helped me fuel my creative fire and keep it burning. It also gave me another writer's perspective on the creative process and the psychology of what it takes to create a work of art.

Then I referred back to one of my favorite books by Steven Covey[26] so I could create the proper habits and mindset that would assist me on the creative journey. The three men, in effect, joined my team to help me produce the book you're reading today. I relied on the giants of the industry – a group that I hand selected to work with me, and you can do the same thing too.

Your team may look a little different than mine, but make sure you have a team of giants on your side. They must encourage you and inspire you; otherwise, kick them off your team because you deserve the very best mentors to travel with you and spur you on.

Leaders can build a team of giants, but they also need relationships with people whom they have physical access. Leaders need help and they are worthy of it, so again – don't be afraid or shameful about asking for help...we cannot be a successful leader without a team.

One of my personal mentors is a leader who I admire deeply. His name is Bob Koenig;[27] he is a professional leadership coach who has been developing leaders for the past forty years. I have learned more from Bob than any other human on the planet. Bob also has a team of giants from which he has learned. He often echoes their words, *"You will be the same person in five years from now, except for the books that you read, and the people you surround yourself with."*

This is a very important idea for us as evolving leaders to understand...simply put, **you will be a product of your team**, the people you surround yourself with, and the other inputs you allow to influence your life. Some of the other inputs might include: media, books, and formal education.

Those who want to continue their evolution must assemble a team of other leaders, coaches and giants who can help take them to the next level.

Remember that leaders are learners and they learn from being proactive about sharpening themselves with knowledge and people.

As leaders we must drink deeply from the fountains of knowledge.

We must build a team of giants, so we can stand on their shoulders.

We must not fear asking for help.

And lastly, leaders must understand that success never happens in isolation, but instead, it is always a team effort.

7. Leaders are Exponential

"Closed minded leaders, close minds."
Andy Stanley[28]

A leader's job is not to produce followers.

A leader's job is to produce more leaders.

The question a leader must ask and answer is, "How can I put myself out of a job by developing new leaders to replace me?"

The insecure leader will never make it to this exponential level.

Mature leaders understand that one of their major purposes is to help develop new exponential leaders. When leaders embrace this idea they also begin to develop further. This becomes a perpetual process of growth. Goethe taught, "*Treat a man as he is and he will remain as* *he is. Treat a man as he can and should be and he will become as he can and should be.*"[29]

The "*Zero Sum Mentality*" is one of the leader's greatest enemies.

This mentality holds that there is only so much credit, fame, promotion, status, customer base and whatever else the insecure leader can think up. The "*Zero-Sum Mentality*" says, "*There will never be enough for me, if someone else also takes credit.*"

The insecure leader thinks of life and opportunity as a pie that has set dimensions with set slices and believes that once that pie is consumed it is gone forever. The "*Zero-Sum Mentality*" produces insecure leaders who reject the idea of abundance and giving. Insecure leaders trap themselves in scarcity thinking which produces followers instead of more leaders. This mentality is the opposite of the truth, and it is a mindset that is bound by greed and scarcity. If you struggle with this mindset, the best thing you can do is study how to develop a growth mindset.

An exponential leader's paradigm is the opposite of the scarcity mindset. It firmly holds that we as leaders have endless resources and opportunity. It understands that the pie of opportunity is ever expanding and that our thinking must be expanding and growing also. Coach and Marine Corps Veteran, Frosty Westering says, "*We are either green and growing or ripe and rotting.*"[30]

This statement is true of our mindset and the way we lead.

If we believe opportunity has expired, it has.

If we believe that limitless opportunities exist, then they do.

The growth mindset almost always precedes action, and action is what creates or limits our leadership and success. One of the best resources one can study on the growth mindset is Carol Dweck's book, *Mindset*. In it she explains that, *"The growth mindset is based on the belief that your basic qualities are the things you can cultivate through your efforts, your strategies, and help from others."*[31]

In great depth, *Mindset* breaks down the psychology of success and debunks what the author calls *"The Fixed Mindset."*

Now that we have talked a little about mindset, let's go back to the number one goal of a leader, which is to develop more leaders and not more followers.

A leader becomes exponential when others emulate their leadership. They become exponential by teaching and developing others to lead and here is why: as anything expands, it take more energy. As our bodies, minds, teams, organizations, and as our leadership expands, it requires more energy. The additional energy and thinking and leadership that our organizations and teams need will be best filled by others.

This is how effective organizations grow; they train up new leaders to take on new challenges and responsibilities. Teams and organizations then become a self-perpetuating body of leaders growing exponentially. The worst thing we can do is fill this additional demand with followers. Instead we want to fill these roles with leaders. Leaders have the ability to problem solve, make decisions and act without much oversite or direction. This is far more efficient and produces an organization that reacts quickly to challenges.

Leaders push limits and use their growth mindset to add value to organizations. As leaders create additional leaders everyone benefits. New skills are learned, efficiencies are exploited, and people are developed. Have you heard the old saying that, *"As the tide of the ocean rises, all ships rise?"* This is the truth about exponential leadership. When a new leader is formed, everyone around them benefits.

"Exponential" means to *"become more and more rapid."*[32]

We become exponential leaders by giving our knowledge and experiences to others and helping them become the leaders we know they can be.

So, where does this leave the leaders who effectively put themselves out of a job?

As a leader continues to train and develop others, new opportunities begin to present themselves. As we grow the capacity of new leaders, we simultaneously grow our capacity and give ourselves opportunity for new roles and responsibilities. Exponential leadership becomes a self-feeding growth formula that helps people and organizations flourish.

When we make the decision to become exponential leaders, there are a few pitfalls to be aware of – the first being that sometimes we can want someone else's improvement or growth to happen more than they do, and this is a trap!

We can never want someone to improve more than they want it for themselves. That will simultaneously lead to unfair expectations for them and disappointment for us. Sometimes people are not ready to grow, and we have to be able to recognize that.

We must also be aware of the perfection trap. The perfection trap causes the leader to think, *"Only I can do something because it has to be perfect."*

The perfection trap also leads us to believe, "Something cannot be done until conditions are perfect."

This type of thinking stems from the scarcity mindset, and what we must understand and accept is that the very idea of perfection is an illusion. Perfection does not exist because people, ideas, and action can always improve according to the growth mindset. This type of thinking will prevent us from becoming exponential leaders, so beware of it. Training and delegation are keys to becoming an exponential leader.

A good rule of thumb to use when making a decision to turn over a responsibility is this…

- "Does the person I am considering turning a responsibility over to care about this matter?"

- And, "Are they trustworthy and capable?"

If we can say "*Yes*" to both of these questions, it is likely they can fulfill the expectations around a responsibility. Most importantly we must guard our minds from the idea that if we develop others and give them our roles and responsibilities, we are at risk of losing either position or credit. This is not only self-sabotage, but it will also lead to the sabotage of our people's development. Remember, our job as exponential leaders is to put ourselves out of a job by training and developing others.

A friend who has 40 years in leadership and management experience after reading this commented on it. "*I've always found that when I developed new successful leaders, the credit rebounded to me. Further, as they continued to impress others, it continued to my credit. Several times I've raised people into leadership roles and they have gone on to really great results. My bosses usually gave me credit for that.*"

Developing new exponential leaders is like throwing a boomerang, if you release it right, it always comes back to you. Just like the boomerang, the credit always returns if we are focused on helping our people succeed.

8. The General, Chief and Affection

*"The true soldier fights not because he hates
what is in front of him, but because he loves
what is behind him."*
-G.K. Chesterton[33]

While doing some research in preparation for an interview I
surveyed great military leaders of the past and present. I
stumbled upon a powerful interview with General James
"MAD DOG" Mattis.

> *General Mattis was asked by a young Marine,
> "What is the greatest quality of a leader?"*
>
> *His response was as surprising as it was profound.
> Mattis replied, "One of the greatest qualities of a
> leader is to have affection for their people."*
>
> *He went on to explain, "When leaders have affection
> for their people, their people will go to any length for
> them. They will lay down their life defending their*

leader and will not quit until the mission their leader set before them is accomplished."[34]

The more I thought about this statement from the General, the more it made sense. When a leader shows affection to their people, a bond is created. This bond is reinforced through trials and tribulations. The bond becomes ironclad and unbreakable if it is nurtured.

Through this relational process between a leader showing affection to their people, a shift is made; the follower is no longer loyal to a leader, but instead, they are loyal to a person who loves and cares for them.

> *Mattis was then asked a follow up question that brought this idea to life. The young Marine asked, "What is the range on your knife throwing hand?"*
>
> *His response showed the wisdom of his forty plus years leading and showing affection to his people. Mattis explained, "After a certain number of frontline years, I've moved to the General's Command tent, but because of the bonds I've created with my Marine's – my range is much farther."*
>
> *"My range extends through the private on the front line. It extends through the crosshairs of the sniper's rifle and through the thousands of Marines charging the enemy. My range is only limited by my ability to lead and show affection to others."*

What a powerful lesson! This is the impact of the exponential leader – it shows the ripple effect that one leader can have by investing in others and reinforcing the idea that they are integral to the mission set before them. A leader's words and actions fuel the hearts of their people.

I am also reminded of the way a leader can touch the heart of his people when I think back to my deployment to Iraq.

> *I enlisted in the Navy when I was seventeen and spent my eighteenth birthday in boot camp. My Navy journey was different than most. I spent a year at Naval Hospital Camp Pendleton, and the rest of the time, I was attached to a United States Marine Corps Unit.*

You may be wondering why a Navy person serves with the Marines. The truth is that Marines are a Department of the Navy, (but don't tell my Marine friends I shared this with you.) My friend and Marine Veteran, Josh Cherry likes to remind me, *"Yes the Marines are a department of the Navy – the men's department."*

That's debatable, but back to the point. The Marines do not have their own medical division, so the Navy provides all medical support for them. I thank God for this fact because my time serving with the Marines was some of the most rewarding years of my life. I served as a Navy Corpsman, and I am proud of it. I learned a lot from the Devil Dogs I served with.

> *A few years into my enlistment, the Twin Towers were bombed. Most people who are old enough,*

remember where they were and how they felt when they received the news that the U.S.A. was attacked by terrorists. At the time, I was at Naval Hospital Camp Pendleton. I remember being called into the break room and watching the second plane fly into a building filled with helpless innocent Americans. When I saw what was happening, one of my first reactive thoughts was, "We are going to war!" Like most Americans, I was fired up and ready to make things right by whatever means possible.

Just over 13 months later I arrived in Kuwait to prepare for the Iraq invasion. One of my most lucid and pivotal memories of service was the day I checked into my command in Kuwait. My thought was, "It is very likely that I will die here, so I am going all in."

I was one of six Corpsmen who were in charge of the medical care of 350 Marines. One of the senior enlisted Corpsman was Senior Chief Bagley[2]. He was a "salty"[3] Corpsman who had been on multiple previous deployments, and because of his experience, he was relaxed every time I was around him. He had a refined character about him that exuded his commitment to his people and the mission. His uniform was always on point[4] and he chose to wear black boots instead of the standard desert boots that

---

[2] Name changed to protect the innocent
[3] Navy lingo for "experienced'
[4] More lingo for "cleaned, ironed, and pristine."

most others wore. The problem with black boots was that they had to be polished daily because of all the dust in Kuwait. But Senior Chief didn't care – his were always polished with a mirror finish.

Senior Chief Bagley was a great leader. He and I were both early birds. I would arrive early at the BAS (Battalion Aid Station), only to be beaten to work by Bagley. When I arrived, without fail, he was listening to music and sweeping the plywood floors. As soon as he noticed that I arrived, he greeted me with a huge smile and asked, "How are you Petty Officer Weaver?"

There is a difference between asking how someone is doing and caring how someone is doing. Each time Bagley asked me how I was doing, my reply was, "I am doing good Senior Chief."

But, good leaders can sense when their people are not right. At the time, I was twenty years old. I was also scared for my life but thought that I covered it up well. Senior Chief sensed my fear. He shared stories of the first Gulf War. His stories gave me confidence that I would survive too. His smile and warm concern for how I was doing always gave me the confidence to face each day. I began to look to Senior Chief for strength and confidence, so I made it a habit to arrive early and listen to the wise sage's wisdom.

What I realize now is that Senior Chief Bagley always made me feel safe, and that is exactly what good leaders do. They attempt to transfer their strength to the people following them. Leaders can use their experience to share strength – there is power in story and there is power in making others feel safe. Leaders show people affection and show them that they are important to the mission at hand. When leaders do this, their followers will travel to hell and back for them; they will charge the front lines for the leader who has showed them affection and made them feel like they are worthy.

General "Mad Dog" Mattis and Senior Chief Bagley knew the difference between asking how their people are doing and caring how their people are doing.

Now you know one of the greatest qualities that a leader can show. **Your job is to go out and care for your people.**

Arrive early to talk to your people. Let people know that you are not only with them, but also for them as their leader. We as leaders don't have to be at war to do this. We can make them feel safe by meeting them where they are and showing them how much we care for them.

9. The Two Types of Leaders

"There are two types of people, those who are humble and those who are about to be humbled."
Matt Deggs[35]

One of the best ways to spot a good leader is to look for someone who is secure enough to admit their limitations. A leader who pretends to know everything actually knows little. A leader who has the courage to say, "*I don't know*," is a leader who is secure in their position. They are more concerned about what is right than what is perceived to be right. As one leader puts it, "*Uncertainty exposes a lack of knowledge. Pretending exposes a lack of character….saying 'I don't know' when you don't know is a sign of good leadership. Pretending to know when you don't know is a sign of insecurity. The only person a pretender deceives is himself.*"[36]

It is very hard to rank the different qualities of leadership, but if I were to rank them, humility would be competing for a top spot. As a leader rises, the probability of falling due to pride becomes greater and greater. The stench of arrogance travels fast when a leader forgets the imperative of humility. Pride travels first class: its ticket price is only a quick dance with the devil. Humans have always wrestled with pride. Freud called it "*ego.*" Others call it "*self-righteousness;*" but for us, we will call this destructive force....simply, "PRIDE." It is one of the great enemies of man. Pride's only desire is to walk us to the edge of a cliff and whisper, "*All these years you thought you could only walk the Earth, but I tell you – fly.*"

Pride's sole mission is to crush and humiliate us. Leaders are especially susceptible to Pride's lies. Pride tells us that we are the source of our success, and we – only we could have accomplished all that we have. Pride's mission is to have leaders believe they are the greatest there ever was and ever will be. Once leaders buy into this lie, prideful actions quickly follow.

Have you ever spent time around a person who was caught up in a battle with pride? I have: let me give you a glimpse into what pride looks like.

> *I once met a man who would never miss an opportunity to mention which of his many cars he was driving. During a professional presentation he and I were attending, he left his sunglasses on the entire time, while sitting in the front row of the room*

and staring out the window. He paid the presenter, who worked hard to deliver an important message to the audience, zero attention.

The irony was that the speaker was presenting on how to be a humble leader.

At the end of the presentation, there was a time for each person to stand and introduce themselves and answer three questions: what is your name, what do you do for work, and what are you passionate about. We were given a time limit of thirty seconds.

All was fine until the man in the glasses began. He must have spent five minutes bloviating about himself. He talked about his upcoming trip around the world, about a party he was hosting, about his international business, and love for exotic cars, all while wearing his dark tinted glasses.

This prideful person disrespected everyone in the room because he valued himself and his time over all others.

You have never met this person...except that you have. You have probably had a similar experience to this.

How do these types of people make you feel?

Do they make you feel less of a person?

I hope not!

We should feel sorry for these types of people and try not to judge them. Pride gives off a certain type of stench that repels most others. But unfortunately, some insecure people are temporarily drawn to this kind of individual. They are lured in by Pride and its various cloaks, only to find out they are being toyed with by the same insecurity that has hoaxed the Pride-stricken individual. These unfortunate people are not necessarily bad people, but the Pride that has infected them has taken over like a disease. When Pride is all boiled down and exposed, it is simply a desperate plea for attention to validate one's worth, or to fill a void in one's life.

Conversely, have you ever met the humble leader who has every right to strut around showing off his accomplishments, but decides not to?

This type of leader is grounded and humbled by something much bigger than material possessions.

Have you ever spent time with someone who has had massive success, but instead of talking about themselves, they desire to learn about you?

This is the way of a humble leader.

Humble leaders separate their accomplishments from their identity. They are secure inside, and outside. These leaders look at their success not as a trophy to show off but instead as a gift that they must steward well.

The main difference between the humble leader and the prideful leader is that the humble leader places a high value on others.

The humble leader knows that people are the most important part of life and that relationships are the key to having a fulfilled life.

The humble leader tries to serve others while the prideful leader has a deep-seated need to be served.

Which type of leader do you want to be around and become?

Make a choice now.

There is a great concept that all leaders should understand. It's a concept from the book *Good to Great*[37], which is one of the best business leadership books of the last few decades. It is the concept of the *Window and the Mirror*.

This concept teaches leaders how to deal with success and failure in a simple binary way. This can be a very useful tool, especially in dealing with success and failure in the public eye. But it is also a great litmus test for our own pride as a leader.

This concept says that whenever a leader experiences a success, they should go and look out the metaphorical *window* and give that credit away to their team.

By default, the credit for success almost always goes to the leader, so it is our job to take a good hard look out the *window* at our team and reallocate credit where it is due. This means that as we experience success we should give it away as much as possible. Not only does this feel great for the leader, it also helps build up our team and apportion credit to those who may otherwise go unnoticed.

Conversely, when a leader and their team experiences a failure, the leader should go to the metaphorical *mirror* to search for the reason why it happened.

I can attest that I have found that this is against our own nature, which is self-preservation. But if you will trust the concept, the entire team will benefit from it.

Looking in the mirror when a failure occurs is especially helpful when the reason for the failure cannot be directly related to the leader. It helps the leader identify blind spots in their own general communication, training and overall leadership. It keeps leaders from causing damage to others, and it keeps leaders focused on the only true thing that we can control – ourselves. This is a valuable concept that will help a leader preserve their team and refine themselves.

Remember, when leaders experiences success, they go to the *window* to shout out accolades to their team, but when they experience a failure, they go to the *mirror* to self-reflect and ask the question, "*What could I have done differently, as a leader, to have prevented this failure?*"

Leaders should be humble and outward focused not only for the good of their team, but also for their own good.

When leaders focus on giving credit away to their team, they simultaneously retain their very best people.

One of the worst days a leader can experience is the day one of their best team members turns in a bitter resignation letter. Giving the credit away to others will limit the number of times that this happens to you.

When we apportion credit to others, their value to the team is reinforced. It isn't hard to understand why. At the core of every human being is a need to feel important and know that they are valued. This is not just some corporate point system that needs to be counted… This is actually a deep and profound biological need that each of us desires to have filled. People long to know they are valued and they are creating value.

One of our greatest human needs is to be told, "*YOU MATTER, YOU ARE IMPORTANT, YOU ARE NEEDED.*"

Leaders need to be humble and secure enough to share these very important statements with their people.

> "*The deepest principle in human nature is the craving to be appreciated.*"
> William James[38]

When is the last time you affirmed the value in others through appreciation?

If it has been more than a week, I challenge you share some appreciation today.

Notice the power that your words have on someone who needs them.

People come alive when they feel valued. There is a kindling of a fire that is started when you encourage people and give them the appreciation they are longing for.

As leaders it is our responsibility to start a fire in the hearts of our people and continue to stoke that fire.

When people are valued and on fire, organizations come alive, teams thrive and relationships are fortified.

There is a second part to this concept that should not go unexplained, and that is "*Accountability.*"

Since the focus of the book is on evolving ourselves as leaders, it is mostly internally focused, but it would be incomplete if we did not discuss accountability.

A leader can take the ultimate responsibility for a failure while simultaneously holding their team accountable.

Just as success is not a one-person show, failure is much the same, and most often, it takes a team to fail.

Accountability should always start within the leader, but then it is also important to do what is necessary to prevent future failures. This starts with the leader owning what they as a leader did wrong, and then asking the people around us to step up and do the same. If we have surrounded ourselves with the right team and are actively setting the example, we will have no shortage of others stepping up to take accountability for issues that go wrong. It is a sign of a problem if nobody else does.

Leaders who lack humility have a closed mindset.

They reject collaboration, limit transparency, lack communication, value process over people, and are limited by their own plateaued thinking. They say things like, *"If you don't like the way I do things, you can find a new job."*

But the leader who lacks humility constructs their own demise because the team or organization that surrounds them will ultimately take on their most significant characteristics, and Pride is potent. Teams will always be a reflection of the humility or lack thereof that their leader possess. This is why humility is so important to ingrain in the culture of everything we do, and why the saying, *"Pride goes before a fall,"* rings true with leaders, followers and organizations alike. Leaders who lack humility will ultimately offend and drive away the most important ingredients to their success – their best people.

10. Connection

*"Leaders worth following are always careful.
They are careful because they genuinely care
for those who have chosen to follow. A leader
who is careless will eventually be considered
thoughtless by those who have entrusted their
future to him."*
Andy Stanley[39]

Leaders should be *for* and *with* their people.

Both of these words *for* and *with* are important, because there are many leaders who are *for* their people but lack being *with* their people. There is something sad but true about human nature and that is, when there is no connection between people, their natural assumption is negativity.

Let me explain....I have friends spread throughout the country. I have very important people in my life, and if I do not hear from them for a while, I naturally begin to think badly...."*Well they must not want to have a relationship with me.*"

In this example, it is just as much my responsibility to stay in contact with them as it is theirs. I especially become more and more negative if I have attempted to contact them and they fail to return the contact. It is my natural inclination to think negatively when there is a lack of connection with the people I have a relationship with.

The relationship between leaders and followers is even more dynamic than my friendship example.

One of the main responsibilities of a leader is to provide connection through communication. People want to know they are moving in the right direction for the right reasons and this takes communication from the leader.

But, there is always an invisible or unstated hierarchy between a leader and their people. This is an implicit barrier between the leader and their people. As a result, it is always more natural for the leader to send communication than for the follower to request information. This fact creates an imperative for a leader to communicate with their people. If a leader fails to be *with* their people either physically or by way of some type of communication, their people will naturally default to thinking negatively. *"Well maybe I am not important enough to have a connection with my leader."*

As a team or organization grows in size or complexity, it becomes harder for the leader to stay connected with their people, but it can be done.

One way this can be accomplished is through the leader pushing communication. There are simple formats that can be used to share pertinent information with the team without overwhelming them. The objective is to stay connected. A leader's communication to their team is for the benefit of their team and it can be simple as writing a weekly email that gives them a few high-level bullet points and also encourages them by sharing credit with team members, or others.

Another way a leader can stay connected to their people is through what the Navy calls, *"Deckplate Leadership."*

The idea is simple but powerful. It's when a leader leaves their office and roams about the organization with the sole objective of connecting with their people.

The highest-ranking enlisted person in the Navy is the MCPON (Master Chief Petty Officer of the Navy). In 2007 the MCPON was Joe Campa. This is how he described leadership, *"Deckplate leadership is a very basic concept. When I am talking to chiefs about it, I am talking about their connection with their sailors. As chief petty officers, that is what give us our credibility with our leadership – knowing our Sailors and knowing the tone of the command so we can best provide input."*[40]

Another way to create connection is for the leader to hold organization-wide *"town hall meetings."* This is where the leader gathers all their people together to openly discuss what's taking place in the organization. This type of connection helps remove barriers and hierarchy structures from an organization, because it levels the access to the leader for everyone. It signals that everyone is equally valuable and that the leader wants to share information with and hear from everyone.

Whatever method you decide, just remember that when there is a lack of connection between the leader and their people, the people naturally default to negative assumptions. They simply go negative.

Why do people go negative?

I believe that it goes back to a fundamental need for us to feel important, and for each of us to feel important, we need some type of connection.

Why is this?

Because we were built for connection.

Disconnection hurts us deeply. It makes us feel insecure. So to make sure our people are not hurt from disconnection, we as leaders need to do everything we can to connect and communicate with them.

This is so important!

Pay attention here leaders, and if you need to be reminded of this, do what I do – set a weekly calendar appointment that says, "WEEKLY TEAM COMMUNICATION."

This is a simple reminder that can keep us from losing the hearts of our team due to disconnection.

11. The Power of Wise Counsel

"A defining moment in our life is when we no longer view asking for help as a sign of weakness, but instead as strength."
Terry Weaver

A mentor of mine, Bob Kapp, has spent over three decades developing leaders. He often reminds those he is mentoring, *"We will be an average of our five closest friends."*[41]

It is true that we take on characteristics of the people who we associate with. I believe this advice is some of the wisest I have ever received. Just think about teenagers! Their parents are always concerned about who they associate with because of what that can do for their future.

We can associate ourselves with leaders through books, podcasts, seminars, TED Talks, and a host of other modern technologies including MOOC's (Massive Open Online Courses). We have the ability to tap into the collective habits, principles, and thought leadership of wise counsel that is made available to us through ubiquitous sources.

Can I suggest that we have the blueprints to *Evolve as a Leader* right in front of us?

We have countless tools at our disposal. All we have to do is pick them up and begin to put them to work. I surround myself with great people of the present, but I also learn from great leaders of the past. I do not let life, death, time, or space keep me from learning from the greatest leaders of all time. I have personally learned from Jackie Robinson, Andrew Carnegie, George Washington, Leonardo Da Vinci, Abraham Lincoln, Martin Luther, and Jesus Christ. These leaders of the past have become my wise counsel. They speak to me and tell me what they have done to become successful. They also show me how a legacy is created and how a leader can be so impactful during their short life, that they make a ripple effect through time. These leaders are humble servants who purposefully left enough of themselves in history so that you can learn from them and add them to your list of mentors. They're willing to counsel you if you are willing to seek them out and search their hearts and minds.

Andrew Carnegie[42] is one of my favorite past leaders for many reasons.

> *He immigrated to the United States from Scotland at a young age, and grew up as the son of a preacher. He grew up without much, but Carnegie made a*

decision to learn, and work hard at an early age. He began his working life as a letter courier, then moved on to a career in the railroad, and finally into steel manufacturing.

At each step, Carnegie got new responsibilities and his leadership grew more widely respected. He was careful with his money and invested it with great care. Carnegie built the giant company that is known today as U.S. Steel, but at the age of sixty-six in 1901, he sold it to J.P. Morgan for $480 million, ($14.1 billion in 2017 dollars).

From 1900 - 1919 Carnegie became one of the greatest philanthropists in the world. He effectively educated a generation by building 2,509 public libraries that offered free learning, all over the country. Carnegie also gave $2 million to establish the Carnegie Institute of Technology, now named Carnegie-Mellon University. He built Carnegie Hall and also funded the construction of 7,000 church organs. This is just a small portion of Carnegie's impact. In total, he amassed and gave away $76.9 billion in today's dollars.

Why did he do this?

Some of the famous words he left behind clue us in on his why:

> *"The man who dies…rich…dies disgraced."*[43]

Carnegie believed that people were the most important element of his business. He valued human potential and built a library in his steel factory, so that his people could educate themselves while they were employed at his company. While speaking of his ideas and the value he placed on people, he commented,

> *"You develop people the same way you mine gold. When you mine gold, you have to move tons of dirt to find one ounce of gold. But you don't go in there looking for the dirt. You go in there looking for the gold."44*

When Carnegie found someone who was willing to work hard and devote themselves to personal growth, he invested in them through leadership opportunities. Over the course of his life's work, Carnegie helped produce forty-three millionaires in addition to the thousands of institutions he established.

But how did he do so much in one lifetime?

Carnegie attributes his massive success to conquering fear and maintaining wise counsel. He was one of the first to formalize the idea of looking to a group of leaders from the past as wise counsel. He assembled twelve leaders into what he called a "*Mastermind Group.*" His wise counsel included the likes of past presidents and leaders. His reason for building a team of wise counsel, he noted, was taken directly from Christ. He explains, *"God in His infinite wisdom created us for relationship, and without the aid of other minds, our thinking is incomplete."*[45]

Whether you believe in Scripture or God, there is wisdom in this idea.

Many people believe asking for help in any form from others is a weakness. But the truth is that when you open yourself up to assistance from others; your thinking and resources become infinitely greater than your own. So leaders must answer for themselves the million dollar question, *"Is asking for help a strength or weakness?"*

When we ask for and receive help, our thinking becomes multi-faceted and pervasive. When we ask for help in any fashion, we gain the strength and wisdom that resides in the others whose counsel we seek. When Andrew Carnegie was asked how he amassed his fortunes and success, *"He attributed his entire fortune to the power he accumulated through this Master Mind."*[46] That is what he called his wise counsel.

Leaders from the past can encourage us and teach us if we tap into their proven ways of thinking.

> *Jackie Robinson[47] is one of many leaders who has taught me to disregard color when looking at people. He has also taught me that when someone or something attacks us, we do not have to attack back. Jackie was honorable when he was given draft*

notice to join the military. He served his country even though he was discriminated against.

He held his ground when his military superiors tried to set him up for failure. Robinson turned to the NAACP for help and was rejected. After a hard fought battle, because of Jackie's faith, he was honorably discharged from the United States Military.

Jackie's military trial paled in comparison to what he went through to become a professional baseball player. Under the most severe discrimination, he believed in and exhibited respect. He made sure that the criticism from others never defined who he was. In the end, his character as a leader won and it's what made him most remarkable.

In 1984 Jackie Robinson was posthumously awarded the Medal of Freedom for his courage and example on and off the baseball field. Jackie died in 1972 but still teaches many leaders today.

12. Preparation and Commitment

*"I will study and prepare myself, and someday
my chance will come."*
Abraham Lincoln[48]

Abraham Lincoln[49] and George Washington[50] are great
teachers, and one of the greatest leadership lessons they
can teach others is that it is never too late to begin to leave
a legacy. George Washington was forty-three years old
when he agreed to become the great military commander
that he is known for today. It was because of his decision at
age forty-three, that he went on to become one of the
greatest military leaders and Presidents of all time.

President Lincoln lost his first political race in 1832 at the
young age of twenty-three. It took him twenty-nine years to
win the office of president, and at the age of fifty-two, Lincoln
began a four year journey that would place him in the history
books as one the greatest leaders and defenders of freedom
our country has ever seen.

It is never too late to begin your leadership journey—if you need convincing, look to the leaders who have gone before you. We can never rewrite our story, but we can always start a new chapter, and that new chapter begins with preparation and commitment.

Both Abraham Lincoln and George Washington became president later in their life, but they shared a very similar discipline early on. Lincoln and Washington were relentless in their preparation and commitment. They prepared all their life for the positions they would eventually be appointed to. Lincoln was known for his preparation and once remarked, *"I will study and prepare myself, and someday my chance will come."*[51]

Many leaders have the formula for success backwards. They believe that if an opportunity presents itself, they will do everything they can to prepare to be qualified for it. **But history shows that preparation precedes the greatest opportunities.**

It has been said that fortune favors the bold, and it does, but according to the great leaders of the past, fortune favors those who are constantly preparing for the opportunities that may present themselves. One of the great leaders of the past who constantly prepared was our first president, George Washington.

Washington, as a young man, was intrigued by his older brother Lawrence who was a military man, a member of the

Virginia legislature and a person of influence. Washington made a decision in his teens to begin his preparation for future opportunities. *"George threw himself into learning proper etiquette, reading serious books, dressing properly, and improving his character."*[52] Because of his dedication to personal preparation, at the age of twenty-one, he was appointed as a commander in the Virginia Militia.

At the time of his preparation, Washington had no idea that he would later in life be approached by The Continental Congress to become the Commander of U.S. Forces for the Revolutionary War. Because of his extensive and constant preparation, Washington was the first choice to lead the war efforts that would eventually enable the independence of the United States.

Leaders need to constantly prepare themselves for the possible appointments their futures hold. Lincoln and Washington made a decision to prepare and because of it, they will be forever remembered as two of the greatest presidents and leaders of all time. Something beautiful and amazing happens when we make a commitment to live a life of preparation. Power begins to flow into our being as a consequence of our preparation; W.H. Murray, the British Highlander and writer explains:

> "Until one is committed, there is hesitancy, the chance to draw back. Concerning all acts of initiative (and creation), there is one elementary truth, the ignorance of which kills countless ideas

and splendid plans: that the moment one definitely
commits oneself, then Providence moves too.
All sorts of things occur to help one that would
never otherwise have occurred. A whole stream of
events issues from the decision, raising in one's
favor all manner of unforeseen incidents and
meetings and material assistance, which no man
could have dreamed would have come his way.
Whatever you can do, or dream you can do, begin
it. Boldness has genius, power, and magic in it.
Begin it now."[53]

Preparation is the currency that we use to make transactions with the future and all that it offers. When we commit to readying ourselves, our capabilities expand, and when our capabilities expand – opportunities follow.

Recently, I spent some time interviewing one of the most engaging public speakers I have ever listened to. Dr. Todd Dewett Ph.D.[54] has authored multiple books, he's an instructor for a global e-learning platform, and an educator of executives and teams for some of the most well-known companies in the United States, including Exxon, Boeing, Microsoft and General Electric. He also holds a Ph.D. in Management from one of the largest universities in the country. I was impressed by the amount of success that Todd has been able to attain on various platforms – speaking, teaching, writing...etcetera, so I began to ask him how he did it all.

When we got into the interview, I was surprised with some of his answers to my questions. Todd shared that the most valuable thing that his eight years of education taught him was that he knew so little. He explained that he continues to prepare daily through reading and various learning techniques, so that when an opportunity presents itself, he is ready. When I pressed him for specifics, he simply said, *"I sharpen my skills by reading, speaking and writing often, so when the phone rings, I am ready."*[55]

The importance of preparation cannot be overstated, and I would suggest that the mindset of leaders who prepare proactively is what sets them apart from those waiting for an opportunity to fall out of the sky.

The difference between a dreamer and a visionary is that the visionary puts action behind their dreams.

Commit to preparing today and watch as opportunity begins to march toward you!

13. Leaders & Battle

"There is a great battle that lies ahead of every leader. History warns us of it, and courage through the battle refines us."

Terry Weaver

I would be remiss and this book would be incomplete, if a section on the *"Leader's Battle"* was not included.

We as leaders must prepare not only for opportunity but also for our greatest battles. All leaders have battles – they are a part of the leadership deal. I had the great opportunity to listen to retired U.S. Army General Stanley McChrystal speak about leadership.[56]

The best way to describe McChrystal is that he is some blend of modern warrior, rock star leader, and humble scholar.

When we met him, he introduced himself,
McChrystal: "Hi my name is Stan."

Me: "Thanks for your many years of service and
your leadership General McChrystal."

McChrystal: "Thanks for your kind words."

Then in front of a crowd of roughly three hundred listeners eager to learn, he shared some thoughts on leadership. He explained the importance of preparation. Then he talked about its significance through a story about one of his greatest foes, Abu Musab Al-Zarqawi.

He is the man who helped lead and develop one of
the greatest, and I say "greatest" with disdain,
modern terrorist organizations the world has ever
known, ISIS. Stan explained that Al-Zarqawi decided
at an early age to become an extremist militant and
began preparing at an early age. Zarqawi began
fighting at the tail end of the Soviet / Afghan war. He
later planned an attack on Israeli forces that landed
him in prison, a perfect place for him to solidify his
extreme nature and further his preparation as a
jihadist leader.

While imprisoned, Zarqawi began to regret some
past decisions which included tattoos on his body. So,
to show his extreme commitment to preparing as a
Jihadist, he began to cut the tattoos out of his skin.
His identity, reputation and commitment to doing
anything that it takes only grew stronger while he
was imprisoned.

Fast forward to May 7, 2004, the day that Zarqawi's preparation culminated into one of the most bloody and savage displays mankind has ever seen. This man who had been preparing most of his life to go to any extent necessary to forward his extreme conviction, beheaded an innocent American contractor in front of a video camera, and then made it public for the world to see. Fear struck the hearts of people throughout the world upon seeing his savagery.

General McChrystal explained that upon watching this video, with clenched fists, he vowed to find and destroy Zarqawi.

Leaders must understand that as they prepare for the future, **there is a dark side to leadership**, and that is the battles that all leaders will face.

Our enemies are also preparing with a heart full of rage that burns to keep the passionate pursuit of victory alive in their mind. We may not be preparing for a military battle, but we are all preparing for some type of battle.

Our foe may come in a different form than General McChrystal's. Some of us will fight a negative mindset or a toxic person in our life. Some will battle cancer or the loss of a loved one. No matter what type of battle it is we must prepare, so that when we are faced by our foe, we are ready for battle.

Overcoming obstacles and problem solving is one of the leader's main functions. **The best types of leaders accept that they will battle on many fronts, so they consciously make a decision to be battle ready**. They train their mind, body, and soul so that when they are hit with a challenge they are prepared to go on an offensive attack against whatever stands in front of them.

As we train and prepare, we can teach our people how to live proactively – living proactively is in essence preparation for offensive measures. Proactive leaders never rest on what they know, they are always seeking out new strategies to charge the proverbial hill.

Leaders are best equipped when they have a battle mindset. One way to know if we are preparing well for the battles to come is to think back over the last week and ask ourselves, *"Did we learn something new – either by reading, or taking a class, or getting in front of some type of expert?"*

If we constantly assess and refine our battle plan, we will be ready to take on the challenges that come our way.

This may sound very militaristic and that's because, leadership is battle. We can take notes from the greatest military leaders and forces of history. There is a positive correlation between the greatest militaries of history and their preparation.

The only reason the U.S. Military is the greatest fighting force on the planet is because of their constant state of battle preparation. All the U.S. Military does is prepare for battle. They explore ways to win battles constantly....day after day, they simulate wartime, and night after night, they prepare for what could come their way. This is called *"Battle Ready Preparation."* If a leader will maintain this type of mindset, they will be in the very best condition to go to war, or solve problems, when it is time.

14. The Foundation

*"Everyone thinks of changing the world, but no
one thinks of changing himself"*
Leo Tolstoy[57]

**"*Character*" is what gives leaders staying power in the
hearts and minds of their followers.** Our character is who
we are as a person. It is the very fabric that guides us and
allows us to make choices. It's what defines us and it is
usually the first thoughts that come to the minds of others
when our name is mentioned.

Leadership has been and will always be first an inside job.
Leadership is a continual uncovering of what dwells inside
the leader. The Evolving Leader explores their heart and
mind to reflect on the state of their own being. They
recalibrate continually to make sure their motives are pure
and their egos are in check. Before leaders can make an
external impact, they must be able to perform an internal

check-up to diagnose and repair any chronic issues of the heart.

When leaders have done a full inventory of their personal drives, have made necessary changes, and have received a clean bill of health, then and only then, are they ready to move on to leading others. There are no shortcuts or detours around this internal step, so leaders need to place a great importance on it!

Have you heard the saying, "*It takes a lifetime to build a reputation, but it only takes five minutes to destroy one?*"

This truth is somewhat unsettling, especially when we realize that we are all flawed and subject to making mistakes. I have made plenty of mistakes that have set me.

It should be comforting to know that while writing our story, we cannot erase the past, but at any time, we can decide to start a new chapter. Each of us have an amazing ability to start fresh whenever we choose to. This should give leaders hope, and while this is true, we should also constantly be on guard against making devastating mistakes. We can stay on guard by learning from those who have gone before us and uncovering the things that were at their core that made them great leaders.

What is at the core of a great leader?

Can we look across the wide spectrum of leaders throughout history to find distinguishable links between them?

Can we find the irreducible minimums for what makes a great leader, and make the claim that – if leaders don't have certain qualities, they will not evolve to their fullest capability?

Can we look at the leaders who have fallen from greatness, and identify what cracked inside of them?

The answer to these questions is, unequivocally, YES!

James Hunter, author of the *Servant,* explains, *"Leadership has little to do with your style (personality) and everything to do with your substance* (character). General Norman Schwarzkopf (pretty much a legend in the U.S. Army) flatly asserts, *'Ninety-nine percent of leadership failures are failures of character.'"*[58]

> *When I was fresh out of college, I landed a job selling 'Big Rigs' a.k.a. Semi-Trucks or Eighteen Wheelers. I went to work selling one of the highest quality trucks on the market at the time: Peterbilt®. During my training I had to learn all that I could about the capabilities of the trucks and what made them the best on the market. I studied everything from their tire tread, to the engine blocks, to the 'huck bolts' that held the cabs of the trucks together.*

I found it very interesting that the strength of these trucks rested on one specific part from which everything else gained its strength, and stability. Some of the trucks were capable of hauling millions of pounds. When all the thousands of parts that it takes to build a modern Semi

Truck are accounted for, the core of the strength is derived
from the truck's frame. It's not from the powerful diesel
engine or any other complex part of the truck, but simply the
metal spine that runs the length of the truck.

> *When I used to sit and engineer these trucks for*
> *customers, I started the process by asking, "What*
> *will it be used for?"*
>
> *I then asked, "How much weight will be placed on*
> *the truck?"*
>
> *Once I knew how much pressure, the load or*
> *downward force, would be placed on the truck, one*
> *of the first things I would specify for the build was*
> *the frame of the truck. Each frame had a rating that*
> *was given by a test of the steel that it was forged*
> *from. The rating that it was given by the factory was*
> *called the "RBM," or "Resisting - Bending - Moment."*
> *It told us how much weight the core of the truck*
> *could handle. The frame of those trucks can be*
> *compared to the character of a leader.*

All leaders have a breaking point. I could list many leaders
who have broken under pressure. You would know the
names of them because they are very public figures. There
was one reason why they broke, and that was because, at
their core, there was not enough strength to withstand the
pressure of their circumstances. Just like the core of the
truck – the frame, leaders also have a frame that holds all

the pressure and demands of life, and that frame is their character. M.H. McKee put it best when he said, "*Integrity is one of several paths. It distinguishes itself from others because it is right, and is the only path upon which you will never get lost.*"[59]

Character is a leader's true North. It's their guide posts. Character keeps us from derailing when we are caught in the storms of life. Dr. Henry Cloud says, "*Who a person is will ultimately determine if their brains, talents, competencies, energy, effort, deal-making abilities, and opportunities will succeed.*"[60]

Integrity demands consistency across one's life. Leaders have different roles, but at their core should be an integration of their most deeply held values.

The opposite of integrity is deception and compartmentalization. When a leader begins to compartmentalize their characteristics and the way they interact with others based on what role they are playing, they begin to deceive themselves and others. The gap between who leaders are in private and who they are in public needs to be held together as closely as possible or it will quickly become an insurmountable chasm. As soon as a leader sacrifices integrity to attain something that looks more important, they have chosen deception over reality. Great leaders fall when they begin to justify deception in their integrity.

Walt Disney[61] is a prime example of what can happen to a leader when they begin justifying who they can be in different areas of their life. Disney was an upstanding figure on stage and in front of the camera, but he became a different person behind the scenes. The gap between who he was in different spheres of his life became dualistic in nature. In their book, *"Leaders, Myth and Reality,"* the authors profile Disney in a conversation he had with a friend that shows just how different he became in his two lives: *"I am not Walt Disney. I do a lot of things that Walt Disney wouldn't do. Walt Disney doesn't smoke; I smoke. Walt Disney doesn't drink; I drink."*[62]

In that conversation, Disney admitted that he was two different characters, one in the public eye – and the other behind closed doors. But for Disney, the duality in his character was much more divisive than just smoking and drinking off stage.

Disney began to widen the gap between who he was to the fans and the leader he was to his employees and those closest to him. Walt Disney's integrity began to crack – he tried to intimidate and control his people instead of giving them respect and autonomy. Walt….in one instance called Ken Anderson, one of his animators, in for a stern tongue lashing, *"If you're thinking of making a name for yourself, then you'd better get the hell out of here now, because the one thing we are selling here is 'Walt Disney'."*[63]

It seems that Disney began to live life through different characters of his choosing. On camera, Walt orchestrated the creation of fairy tale environments…. This was the same person who brought Mickey Mouse and Cinderella into creation. When the public eye saw him, Walt was all smiles – he communicated a message of joy and fantasy, but behind closed doors, he looked much more like one of the villains from his stories.

Disney's disintegrated character ultimately led to an employee strike, a divorce, and trail of carnage personally and professionally. Later, in a House Committee testimony, Walt Disney would sum up the reason for much of his business troubles to communist interference and ungrateful workers.[64] It's true Disney made many mistakes, just as all leaders make mistakes, but Disney's mistakes were a culmination of decisions to sacrifice integrity for short gains. When integrity is sacrificed, a leader's demise is almost always eminent. When a leader's integrity fails, relationships, processes, and lives begin to crumble.

If you're reading this section on "Character," and saying to yourself, "*Well….I've made too many mistakes to be a leader.*" It's simply not true. Leaders make mistakes, because they are human.

I have made big mistakes. At times my character was not strong enough to withstand the pressures of life. My character was flawed, and it was no fault but my own. It took me a long time to recover, and I had to do a lot of learning, but it was possible only by placing the utmost importance on my character integrity. When I reflect on the time when my character crumbled and the time it took to rebuild what I sacrificed, I often say to myself, "*I paid a price, but I am much better because of my lessons learned.*"

It's important for leaders to know that they can rebuild. When we get knocked down, even if we are the ones doing the knocking, we can always choose to get up, make course corrections and learn from our mistakes. **The only true mistake is the one that is not learned from.**

One of my favorite stories that illustrates this point is of the young Abraham Lincoln.[65]

> *Just after Lincoln became a practicing lawyer, he began writing open letters about people he disliked. He wrote about one of his foes who happened to be a politician named James Shields. Mr. Shields became infuriated and decided to challenge Lincoln to a public sword duel to the death. Lincoln agreed and began to prepare for the fight. Lincoln, being the consummate preparer, took sword fighting lessons from high level fencing coaches, but deep down Lincoln was scared. He did not want to fight and regretted his mistake of writing the condemning letters. But Lincoln's pride would not let him back down from the challenge.*
>
> *On the day of the duel, both Lincoln and Shields stood ready to fight, but just before they began, their assistants pleaded with them to not move forward.*

Eventually, they both agreed to call off the fight. The day was a pivotal learning lesson for young Lincoln. This mistake helped Lincoln adjust a crucial flaw in his character. It was this day that Lincoln decided that he would never again openly criticize those he did not agree with. He made a decision to become a person of integrity in public and private.

My hope is that this book will help leaders make necessary character adjustments and that it does not take a near death experience for them to identified and made.

When leaders make mistakes of any size, they must reflect on them and make a decision to put safeguards in place to never allow them to happen again.

A mistake of any size is an opportunity for growth and learning.

15. A Leader's Judgement

"To handle yourself, use your head; to handle others, use your heart."
Eleanor Roosevelt[66]

I was excited when I heard a guest speaker was coming to town who was an esteemed professor from a large and well-known university. I was eager to learn from this person because of his accomplishments, his national notoriety, and because he was "different." I first learned about him by seeing some national press that he gained for the kindness he showed to one of his students. His empathy for a student who felt alienated due to her circumstances caused her to instead feel welcomed and included. His actions warmed the hearts of our nation and mine too.

From the moment the professor walked on the stage, I knew that his talk was going to be engaging and dynamic, and over the next twenty minutes I found myself enthralled with his words. But I also found myself deeply offended because of some of the things he said. He started his talk by listing all that was wrong with the American culture today. He stated that the "U.S.A." did not stand for the "United States of America," but that it actually stood for the "united states of arrogance." He remarked that our country's missionaries need to slow their roll and instead of handing out shoes in Africa and then patting themselves on their backs, they needed to get to know the people. He ended by saying that when others kneel to protest the American Flag, he kneels with them to fight for justice.

As the professor said these things, a small fire lit in my chest, and it began to burn hotter and hotter. As I listened to him, I became very angry.

There was something that was triggered inside of me. He challenged some of my core beliefs, and I let myself become offended by what he said. This was the first time in a long time that I felt I was losing control of my emotions.

After his talk was finished, people swarmed him to thank him for his talk. I was sort of beside myself over what just took place. I felt a strong desire to share that I did not agree with most of what he said, but I waited. I thought more about my emotions and why I was so offended, and what I might say to him. I was eager to share my thoughts, so the next day I found his information and sent him an email detailing all the things that I disagreed with in his talk. I asked if we could meet up. He agreed, and we set a date.

I drove for several hours to have lunch with him, so I could try to understand why he said the things that he did. When we sat down for lunch on the agreed day, we immediately made a connection by talking about one of our shared affinities – our undergraduate experience at our alma maters. We knew some of the same instructors and shared a few passions.

But after a few minutes of warming up to each other, I shared that I served in the U.S. Military defending the values of our nation in Iraq. I shared that the reason I wanted to sit down with him was to understand more about the things that he said about the country that I loved. I shared that I was personally offended by some of the things he said, but instead of staying offended and judging him, I wanted to learn more about him. I also told him that I believed that as leaders we should try to first seek to understand and then seek to be understood.[67] This idea of seeking first to understand has kept me from judging others too many times to count.

During our lunch, he was very gracious and over the course of two hours, he shared some of his experiences with injustice, racism, judgement, and inequity. He shared that he had been targeted and discriminated against by law enforcement, by business professionals, and even by his own countrymen. He also shared a little about his faith – that he was a follower of Christ, and that he was working to change the way he communicated. He went on to say that he wanted to share more good news but that he was challenged internally because of the problems in our current system.

I won't share the specifics of his story, because they are his to share, but I will tell you that he has experienced some very challenging things in his life that have shaped the way he sees the world and how he interacts with it. As I listened to him, I began to feel a small piece of the pain that he and his family have gone through because they are a different race than I am. I realized that I was born with a degree of fortune and that I never had to experience some of the pain that he has gone through. I also realized that the man who sat across the table from me was a great human being who had a desire to be treated with love and respect.

He shared that one of his greatest joys of being a professor is the time he gets to spend with his students during his office hours. He typically has a line of students waiting to discuss critical life struggles they are going through. His students recognize that he is a caring person, and they can't help but to ask him for advice. When a leader is caring, there is a magnetism that surrounds them, and those who need to be cared for are drawn to them.

The professor shared his love for studying leadership and how to better serve others. He shared some of his favorite scripture with me and why it was important to him. We talked about some of our mutual struggles with religion, life and our past.

Towards the end of our conversation, I told him that after hearing him speak, I judged him prematurely. I also told him that he is a much different person than I misjudged him to be. At the end of our time together, I asked him if we could pray together, and he agreed. I reached across the table and gripped his hand as if we were going to arm wrestle. Over the next few minutes we exchanged prayers for each other; prayers for strength, for wisdom and protection, and prayers for guidance. Just before we got into our cars to leave, we hugged each other and I told him that I loved him; he replied, "*I love you too brother!*"

As I write and reflect about this experience, I get emotional because this experience is so valuable to me….it is one that I will never forget. Every once in a while, we have an experience in our life that marks us forever. This is one of those experiences for me. The very person who I thought was an enemy of some of my closest held values became a friend who I understood and cared for.

Just as my new friend's experiences shaped him, our experiences shape us. Our experiences shape how we interact with the world and with the people we meet. In my case, my experience fighting in a foreign war that took the lives of many Americans, has made me very sensitive to anything that I perceive as disrespect to the flag that stands for values that I hold near and dear to my heart. My experience with a personal savior and great people of faith make me want to defend anything that might harm them.

Each of us wears a pair of metaphorical lenses through which we see life. At times the lenses are very useful. We use them to make judgements, keep ourselves from danger, and guide what we will and will not accept. But at times, they can distort the way we see others. Our environment and negative experiences we encounter in life can create stains on the lenses we see through.

Understand that we will never see things with absolute objectivity.

We all see things through our experiences, which is not bad, just one sided. When I heard the professor speak, I listened to and interpreted his message through my experiences and determined that he was wrong based on my one sided judgement – the lenses I viewed him through. There is a wonderful saying from the Dalai Lama that reminds us, *"Being aware of a single shortcoming within yourself is far more useful than being aware of a thousand in someone else."*[68]

The shortcoming that keeps most of us from seeing others objectively is our natural tendency to see them through our experiences. **The idea of seeking first to understand is an invaluable lesson for leaders to embrace.** When we see or hear something we disagree with, our first action should be to lay down the metaphorical lenses we see through and try to understand more about the source.

Emerson warns, *"People do not seem to realize that their opinion of the world is also a confession of character."*[69]

Our perceptions and opinions, whether complete or not, are a confession of who we are. When we make a snap judgement without first seeking to understand, we trade truth for perception. As leaders, we should be on the side of seeking the total truth, which can only be determined by seeking to find out what is missing from our understanding before we make a determination on a matter.

Every person is different than us in some way, and we should try to learn from them and discover the magic in their uniqueness. We may not agree with others after we have gotten to know and understand them.

I still do not agree with everything my new friend spoke about, but I now appreciate and respect him and the opinions that he holds.

Remember – the next time someone says something that makes your emotions flare up: if you do your best to understand them, you may just make a lifelong friend.

16. Leader or Servant

"Service is the rent we pay for the privilege of living on earth."
N. Eldon Tanner[70]

Leadership and service are inseparable ideas. They reinforce each other and do not compete for superiority. The greatest leaders are in fact the greatest servants. **Great leaders understand that leadership is a form of service.**

When we lead, we must keep the desires of our people top of mind. Leaders realize that their people are the *'most important'* part of their mission. We cannot do a good job of serving our customers without a healthy team. To have a healthy team, we must serve our people before we can serve our customers.

Walt Disney knew that he could not serve his customers without others when he said, "*You can design and create, and build the most wonderful place in the world. But it takes people to make the dream a reality.*"[71]

But somewhere along the way, Walt became disillusioned and lost sight of what was most important. True magic resides in the collaboration of hearts and minds pointed in the same direction working to attain a shared goal. When leaders forget who is most important, their company or team will never create the magic that lies in their collective efforts.

If we want to see our companies flourish, then we must start with the desire to see our people flourish. When a leader desires to see their people flourish, it can be felt by everyone around them. A culture of goodwill is created, and this is what is known as a *"Servant Culture."* It begins to become imbedded in the hearts and minds of our people. When we build a Servant Culture in our team, we no longer have to worry if our customers are being treated fairly, because the culture spreads through us, to our teams, then to our customers.

Leaders in corporate America have taken notice of the power of a Servant Culture coursing throughout an organization, and the smart ones are rapidly changing to make the idea of top down servant leadership a priority.

Chic-fil-A® is the best case study in Servant Leadership. The company embraces Servant Leadership and admits that it's their secret sauce. Mark Miller, VP of High Performance Leadership at Chic-fil-A notes:

> "People are always watching the leader – whether we want them to or not! They are generally looking

for clues regarding what's important to the
leader…..If a leader says something is important,
people expect that person to live like it's important.
The gap between what we say and do as leaders can
be lethal."[72]

The importance that Chick-fil-A places on servant leadership can be felt throughout the organization. I sat down with a friend and fellow Navy Veteran who just received the approval for his second Chick-fil-A franchise. During our lunch, he explained how important the culture of servant leadership is to the company. He shared that when he was getting approved to become an owner operator with the company, they performed a background check in which they contacted kids that he associated with in junior high school. He said the background check was more rigorous than the one he went through to get top secret clearance in the military.

I asked my friend how many employees he has working for him, and he shared, "*Just over seventy*". I asked if he knew all their names and his answer was, "*Yes!*" When I visit my friend's restaurant I usually see him interacting with the customers. He is asking them if he can grab them extra napkins or refills. You would never know that he is the owner of the restaurant because the gap between what he says is important and what he does is non-existent.

I remember the first time I visited my friend's Chick-fil-A franchise. I was served by a young man named Sean. He greeted me very politely, and then he asked me my name while I was at the register. After I ordered, he brought me my food and asked if I had everything I needed. I explained that I was fine, and said thank you. After about ten minutes, Sean circled back around to my table and asked, "*Mr. Weaver, how was your food*?"

I was really surprised by Sean's level of care for me. For a split second I wondered where I was, because in my experience most fine dining establishments do not ask for and intentionally remember people's names when serving them. I was blown away by the attention to detail, and respect that my friend's people showed their customers. It was a testament to the power of a culture built on Servant Leadership.

In an essay written about Servant Leadership, Mark Miller closes a chapter titled *Great Leaders SERVE* this way:

> "If you are looking for the latest techniques in coercing people to do your bidding, you can continue your search. Servant leadership is not for you. It's not a strategy or shortcut to success. However if you are willing to begin the long journey of adding value to others, putting their interests ahead of your own, helping them win....you will enjoy new levels of success, satisfaction, and impact."[73]

An organization known for building one of the greatest service cultures is the great Ritz-Carlton® Hotel chain. Their President echoes the words of Mark Miller. Simon Cooper comments on building a service culture – *"A culture is built on trust. And if leadership doesn't live the values that it requires of the organization; that is the swiftest way to undermine the culture. No culture sticks if it's not lived at the highest levels of the organization."*[74]

The goal of the Ritz-Carlton is to create an extraordinary experience for their guests, and the lengths to which they will go to serve their guests are what continue to raise their servant culture to almost mythic heights. Cooper shares a few examples of what some of his employees did for their guests to make them feel like they were valued:

> "There are stories about hiring a carpenter to build a shoe tree for a guest; a laundry manager who couldn't get the stain out of a dress after trying twice flying up from Puerto Rico to New York to return the dress personally; or when in Dubai a waiter overheard a gentleman musing with his wife, who was in a wheelchair, that it was a shame he couldn't get her down to the beach. The waiter told maintenance, who passed word, and the next afternoon there was a wooden walkway down the beach to a tent that was set up for them to have dinner in. That's not out of the ordinary, and the general manager didn't know about it until it was built."[75]

These examples of servant leadership are sometimes hard to imagine, but they are what has created an impeccable reputation for the Ritz-Carlton. This type of leadership starts with the person at the helm of the ship, and it trickles down to everyone else. John Maxwell is famous for saying, *"Almost everything rises and falls on leadership."*[76]

This certainly seems to be the case for the leaders of organizations such as, Chic-fil-A, and The Ritz-Carlton.

When I think of a servant leader, my friend and mentor Bob Koenig[77] comes to mind. During the first year of launching the VEL INSTITUTE®, a non-profit organization that helps connect and develop Veterans, Entrepreneurs and Leaders, we began holding leadership development studies as a way of helping others grow their knowledge about what it takes to be a great leader. Toward the end of our very first course, I was introduced to Bob. I asked if he would sit in and lead one of the sessions for our course. He agreed, and we decided that he would join us for the tenth session which was also the last of the course.

After sitting through one session under his leadership, I knew that I needed to try to keep Bob engaged with the organization. Long story short, since the day Bob first lead our session, he has continued to return and serve as our program director. Over the past four years, Bob has spent countless hours serving others. Why does he do it? Because he believes in serving others.

Because of Bob's servant leadership and his example, he has been named an honorary founder of the VEL INSTITUTE. There are only a few people I know who serve the way Bob does. He is a consummate gentleman and professional who is focused on continually building others up. I often thank Bob for the many years he has chosen to serve with the organization. Each time I do, he reminds me that his service is not a "*have to,*" but that for him, it is a "*get to.*"

Bob has taught me and many others that one of the distinctions between a *leader* and a *servant leader*, is the way they view what they do. After a couple of months of working with Bob in our programs, he handed me a copy of his favorite book, *The Servant,* and inside the cover he wrote, "*Thanks for serving in so many ways.*"

Servant Leadership is more of a philosophy for living than a style of leadership. It transcends the action of leading and gives us a psychology or a framework to lead through. When someone joins our team, we need to ask ourselves, "*How can I best serve them and help them accomplish the desires of their heart?*"

When we begin to act out the qualities of a servant leader, everything changes. Benjamin Disraeli[78] was elected twice as the Prime Minister of the United Kingdom; he was also the first ethnic minority to hold the office of Prime Minister. We see traces of his leadership in the statements he made. Disraeli advised the people around him that, "*The greatest good you can do for another is not just to share your riches but to reveal to him his own."*[79]

A servant leader asks, *"What am I willing to sacrifice for those who are under my authority?"*

> *One of the greatest acts of humility and servant leadership that I have seen took place on April 13th, 2017. Pope Francis arrived at a penitentiary to visit and encourage the inmates who were incarcerated in Paliano Prison, just outside of Rome, Italy. Some of the inmates were serving 50+ year sentences; while there he bowed down and washed the feet of twelve of them.*
>
> *The twelve inmates included Muslims, Orthodox Christians, Buddhists and other faiths. One by one, he knelt down and poured water on their feet, wiped them clean with a towel and finished caring for them by kissing each of their feet. I could only imagine the way the inmates felt after this happened. They may have felt jubilation, maybe a little unworthy, but If I were in their shoes (or out of their shoes so to speak), I would undoubtedly feel encouraged by Pope Francis. What an incredible lesson in leadership and humility that Pope Francis taught the world that day.*[80]

Servant leaders live a life of continual encouragement.
Encouragement is the action of giving someone support,

confidence, or hope. When I drive my kids to school, I often ask them how their day is going to be. We have talked through the ways that we believe can help our days go right, and one of the ways we have decided on is by encouraging others. I have taught them that when we encourage others, we help put courage into them. It's a way for us to share our strength with others when they need it most.

When we give encouragement and serve others, they receive strength, but so do we. We receive strength in the bond between us and the person with whom we share our strength. As leaders, we have a responsibility to share our strength with others through encouragement. This does not mean we have to wash their feet. What it means is that we should find our own unique way to share strength with those around us.

Dr. Albert Schweitzer[81], a man of incredible accomplishment in a wide spectrum of work including: medicine, music, philosophy and theology, won the Nobel Peace Prize in 1952 for his work – "*Reverence for Life*." While speaking to a group of people, Dr. Schweitzer remarked, "*I don't know what your destiny will be, but one thing I do know. The only ones among you who will be really happy are those who have sought and found how to serve.*"[82]

A very pointed statement from a man who left an indelible mark on history and many lives.

Leaders who end up leaving a legacy behind, at some point in their lives, realize that leadership is about serving others and being a part of something that greatly exceeds themselves. One of the greatest examples of this type of leader is Pat Tillman[83]. Pat was one of the greatest servant leaders of the 21st century. He was a star football player at ASU before being drafted to the NFL in 1998. By the year 2000, he earned a starting position and set a record for the Arizona Cardinals for the most tackles in a season. Pat was loyal to what he held as important and it showed when he passed on a lucrative contract elsewhere, so that he could stay and play for "*his team*". [84]

Pat was deeply affected by the terror attacks on America that took place on September 11th 2001. After much thought, he made a decision to leave a $3 million dollar NFL contract to join the U.S. Army. Pat became an Army Ranger after turning down higher status positions offered from the military's senior officials at the Pentagon. Pat wanted to serve others and defend what he held near and dear to his heart.

I recently spent time talking with a former NFL player who knew Pat. He explained that he was shocked when Pat told him that he was putting his NFL career on hold so he could join the Army and serve his country. He went on to share, *"I didn't know how to respond when Pat told me he was leaving his wife, freedom and a huge contract with the NFL to go fight in a war."*[85]

The story of Pat Tillman, I would argue, is a story of heroism. But from what I have been told by Pat's family and friends, he just saw it as an opportunity to simply defend and serve his fellow people and country. It was his duty as a leader.

I am fortunate that I've been able to get to know such a person like Pat Tillman. I did not get the chance to meet him personally, but nonetheless he has greatly influenced my life. Because of his sacrifice, I have had the opportunity to be impacted by his legacy. In 2004, Pat's widow Marie and a few of his closest friends and supporters established the Tillman Foundation®, an organization that grants scholarships to veterans and family members of veterans. To date, the foundation has granted $16 million to fund 580+ scholars to attend over 100 different universities across the country – the same country that Pat died for. I am honored to be one of the veterans who received the namesake scholarship from the Pat Tillman Foundation.

Since becoming a Tillman Scholar, I have had the opportunity to spend time with some of Marie and Pat's best friends. They shared that Pat used to challenge the people closest to him to grow as leaders by sending them articles via email with the pointed instructions, *"Read this and we will discuss it next time we meet."*

Pat knew that helping others become better was a form of service to them. Pat knew that leadership was about serving others, and while his story is tragic, his legacy will be forever remembered because of the leader he decided to become.

A final thought on servant leadership and encouragement.

Encouragement is a way to serve others.

When people are in need of help, they typically isolate and try to keep their problems to themselves. This is the worst thing that they can do to deal with their problems. For some reason most people see asking for help the wrong way. We see reaching out for help as a weakness.

Instead, we need to see reaching out for help as a way to harness the strength of others. Knowing this, when we see someone isolating and shutting others out, it's our cue to encourage them.

We don't need to have all the details. In fact, we don't need to have any details. As servant leaders, it is our responsibility to communicate that we care for those who need us and remind them that they are not alone.

17. A Leader's Identity

"As a Man Thinketh, So is He."
James Allen[86]

As leaders, it is important to know who we are, but I would suggest that it's even more important to know whose we are.

As leaders, we need to be able to answer the basic questions:

- Who do we belong to?

- Who do we work for?

- Who were we created for?

- What were we created for?

These are all very deep, and often times hard questions to answer. For some it takes a lifetime of searching to be able to answer these questions, but they are questions worthy of wrestling with. Ultimately, leaders should be able to answer these questions, because they help us solidify our identity and direction. Leaders need to know their identity and direction, so they can stand up for what they believe in. Before we lead others, we better know where we are headed and why we are on the journey.

A brilliant ancient proverb sheds light on the importance of direction – it made me stop and think for a while and evaluate my own journey as a leader. It reminds each leader, *"If you do not change your direction, you may end up exactly where you are headed."*[87]

When a leader knows who they are and who they belong to, their identity and direction in life becomes crystal clear. *The Purpose Driven Life*[88] has sold over 33 million copies and has been translated into 50 different languages. The opening line of the book is priceless and a little shocking – it says, *"It's not about you. The purpose of your life is far greater than your own personal fulfillment, your peace of mind, or even your happiness."*[89]

Millions of readers have been able to get past the opening line of the book, because they are searching for their purpose. They are seeking the reason they are here on this earth. They are seeking their identity – who they are and whose they are.

Socrates taught, *"An unexamined life is not worth living"*.[90] This statement is pretty cut and dry and may be a little harsh, but it is worth mentioning because ultimately, the belief in who we are determines our direction. We are all heading somewhere and we can consciously decide our direction, or we can passively travel through life.

> *"If you don't know where you are going, any road will get you there."*
> Louis Carroll[91]

A leader's identity will determine if they are going to float for decades on the sea of mediocrity or charge the hill of transcendence and live a life of purpose.

We could discuss identity and how to find our identity for chapters at length, but a great starting point for determining our identity is to ask ourselves the question: *"What do we value?"*

We can perform an exercise of determining our values by listing the top twenty ideas, people, and things, we hold most dear. Then, place them in rank order, one through twenty. Once we have done this, we can explain why we value each of them by writing a paragraph that explains why we hold them as valuable. This exercise can tell us much about our identity and values, but this book is not intended to help people find their identity, just to explain the importance of it with regard to evolving as a leader.

Remember, it is important for a leader to be able to answer the questions I laid out for you before.

- Who do we belong to?

- Who do we work for?

- Who were we created for?

- What were we created for?

If you need help discovering your identity and coming up with a personal mission, vision and purpose statement, I recommend the book, *Three Big Questions* authored by Dave Phillips. [92]

18. Leaders and Significance

*"The two most important days of a man's life
are the day on which he was born and the day
on which he discovers why he was born."*

Dr. Ernest T. Campbell[93]

Time has a way of teaching leaders to view their life as a race towards significance.

They realize everyone is in a race, but most are racing for a prize with no significant reward. It is my belief that some of the greatest leaders are much more concerned with rewards that can never be monetized, but that can only be felt internally.

Significance is different for everyone.

- Significance for the insecure teen can merely be a compliment from someone of influence.

- Significance for the power-hungry CEO can be a promotion to a corner office and a ten percent raise.

But true significance is greater than status, power and monetary compensation. Looking for significance in external things always leads to a dead-end street.

When our quest for significance is based on the external rewards, we tend to compare ourselves with those around us. President Theodore Roosevelt was brilliant when he said, "*Comparison is the thief of joy.*"[94]

When people look to their bank accounts or titles for significance, it gives them a temporary shot of self-gratification, but it then shortly wears off. Jackie Gleason, the great American comedian, once remarked, "*You know the problem with the rat race is – that even if you win, you're still a rat!*"[95]

Looking for significance in external things is like "*trying to catch the wind*" – it can never be caught. No matter how much status, money or accolades you attain in your lifetime, none of it can be taken with you at the end of your life. I once heard someone say "*Hearses have no hitches.*" A simple but powerful reminder – only that which resides within us can be taken to the grave.

I want to go on record and say there is nothing wrong with making money. It is the idolization of money that can lead us astray. Money is amoral – it is neither good nor bad. It is simply a medium of exchange that we trade time and skill for. Money is a means of subsistence, not significance.

When leaders realize they have options in trading their time and skill, but make an intentional decision to trade them for significance: instead of money or power, a shift towards significance is made.

The leader looks within for significance. As a leader grows in wisdom and age, they begin to see life more and more clearly, because they can look back at their past, and determine what they have been living for. Life is somewhat paradoxical in nature as Søren Kierkegaard notes, "*It is perfectly true, as the philosophers say, that life must be understood backwards. But they forget the other proposition, that it must be lived forwards.*"[96]

Leaders understand they are locked into a race, and they cannot wait until the end of their life to look back and see how they performed. They understand they must use their days to do what is most important, so they can one day look back at their life, and celebrate a life lived significantly.

Leaders begin to realize significance when they spend their time investing in the quality of other's lives. When we add to the lives of others, our lives begin to increase also. Feelings of joy and significance grow out of serving others and helping them achieve their worthy desires in life.

All leaders have a unique gift that can help someone who is struggling. A leader's influence in the lives of others has the ability to mark it forever.

Maya Angelou said it best when she spoke these words, "*I've learned that people will forget what you said, people will forget what you did, but people will never forget how you made them feel.*"[97]

Throughout Maya Angelou's life, we see the significant impact one person can make when they decide to live with purpose. The message she spoke lifted the spirits of millions of people, and despite her personal struggles with discrimination, she somehow found a way to turn hate into love for others. Maya was a leader because she rose above hate, and she chose to reflect love even in the darkest of times. Because of her actions, she was awarded over fifty honorary doctorate degrees from major universities throughout our country. Maya lived to eighty-six years of age, but left a mark on history that will live on for centuries. Angelou's daughter writes of her,

> Maya's "message was one of inclusiveness; that despite our ethnic, religious and cultural differences, we are more alike than unalike. She saw all our differences in language, orientation and perspective as an indication of the richness of our imagination and creativity, and as elements of our nature that we should celebrate. She believed that we are all images of God, no matter how we look or what name we use to call upon the Divine and Sacred Being."[98]

When we look at Maya's life, we see a great example of how one can evolve through periods of struggle – as she was determined against all odds to set an example for others to follow. Maya[99] began her working life early becoming a sex worker, a night club dancer, a fry cook, but she knew that her life was meant for more – so she continued to advance herself. At age forty-one she published, "*I Know Why the Caged Bird Sings,*"[100] a book that went on to become a literary masterpiece and international best-seller. She was named the first Reynolds Professor of American Studies at Wake Forest University. She became the second poet in history to read at a presidential inauguration in 1993, and she worked alongside Dr. Martin Luther King to bring about racial equality.

Maya Angelou embraced the idea of taking personal responsibility to serve others – she once noted, "*Don't just complain about the problems you see and do nothing; roll up your sleeves and get to work finding solutions and remedies. We do a disservice to our children and to the future by not addressing the problems that confront us.*"[101]

Maya's parting advice to humanity was simply, "Pursue the things you love doing and then do them so well that people can't take their eyes off of you."[102]

When leaders pursue something that brings significance to others, their lives are changed for the better. Slowly but surely, the quality of life for a small chunk of humanity becomes enriched. As the significance multiples, the ripple effect from one person living purposefully becomes an unstoppable force of good.

This type of leadership is contagious – when others see it, they want to emulate the leader's actions which only compounds the significance. Maya Angelou inspired so many. One of the humans she inspired is the mighty Oprah. Oprah notes that from the time she opened Maya's book, there was an instant connection. Maya went on to mentor Oprah for twenty plus years and taught her how to replace anger with love. Oprah refers to Maya Angelou as her mother, mentor, sister and friend.[103]

Tyler Perry,[104] was then inspired by Oprah just as millions of others have been. In an interview, Tyler shared that at one point in time he was working at a hotel Oprah was staying at. Tyler positioned himself in a hallway that Oprah had to walk through to enter and exit her room and began vacuuming the carpet and decided to stay there until he saw her. Tyler spent hours working up the courage to ask her for an autograph. Finally, he spotted her leaving the hotel and turned to her to ask for her autograph….she responded by writing a big "O" on a piece of paper. When he reflects on that that day, he calls it a *"good moment."*

Tyler being inspired, worked for years to become a significant leader in film and entertainment. Eventually, Tyler signed a multi-year agreement to work with Oprah. Oprah not only became a business partner with Tyler, but she is also the Godmother of his son.

Can you see the ripple effect that leaders have on others?

Leaders who decided to pursue significance, inspire others to do the same.

The contagious nature of a significant leader opens the hearts and eyes of those around them and spurs them on to serving others passionately.

These are only a few examples of what living significantly can do for and to others.

Our job as leaders is to move towards living more and more significantly and to take as many people with us as possible.

19. The Core of A Leader

*"The final estimate of men shows that history cares
not an iota for the rank or title of man has borne, or
the office he has held, but only the quality of his
deeds and the character of his mind and heart."*

Samuel Brengle [105]

Biologically, everything begins somewhere and ends
somewhere. Everything flows from a source. The source of
one's leadership is their motives, heart, and mind.

Our leadership is built in a linear fashion. Leaders decide
through trial and error that there are good ways to lead, and
there are bad ways to lead. Our goal should be to get to a
place where we are evaluating and reinforcing our identity
as a leader, and then everything else should flow from this
leadership identity.

At the core of any leader is their identity.

Through much effort, myself and a group of wise leaders have identified what factors we believe should be considered when developing one's personal leadership identity, or philosophy.

These specific parts of the leader's core are:

- Mental
- Emotional
- Physical
- Spiritual
- Purpose
- Creativity

Mental

Our mental development is of great importance.

In the simplest of terms, our mental faculty can be compared to an operating system of a computer. The operating system of a computer enables everything else to function. A computer without one is just a collection of parts that can do nothing. The Mental Factor does the same for a leader. It drives our decisions and helps us determine what should be kept, and what should be discarded. It also tries to keep us from danger and does much more.

It's important to understand that we can develop our mental faculty, and as previously discussed, we need to maintain a growth mindset to help us adapt to change.

The day we close our minds to new ideas or ways of thinking is the day we begin to coast toward irrelevance.

Always remember the mind is the workshop for innovation and improvement.

Emotional

Our emotional development should also be cultivated proactively. We should be attempting to grow our emotional understanding and empathy towards others. There has been much written on the value and importance of empathy from which we can learn.

While listening to General McChrystal[106] speak, he said that he looks for two qualities in someone when he is seeking out new leaders to work with. **The first is the ability to make decisions, and the second is empathic leadership**.

It's our emotions that make us human. Many other mammals and creatures have mental faculty, but only humans have the full spectrum of emotions that make us deeply unique and creative. Leaders must be able to understand the emotions of others while simultaneously activating and subordinating their own, so they can compose the proper way of dealing with critical situations.

Physical

The physical development of a leader may be the most forgotten or neglected, but it is one of great necessity. Our body is the vehicle for everything that we do – it's what enables us to lead. Some leaders run their metaphorical gas tank on empty until they are stalled out on the highway of life by a physical issue.

Our daily regimen should include some type of physical fitness that helps keep our vehicle, our body tuned up. Some believe they do not have enough hours in the day to work out, but I would suggest the opposite. We don't have time to ignore our bodies.

There was a time when I neglected my body, because I was quote, too busy to exercise. Finally, I moved out of self-deception and into seeing exercise as a must, so I returned to the gym.

> *While there, I saw a friend of mine, Tommy. His questioning began. Tommy was a Marine at one time, and Marines have a way of remembering just how important it is to exercise even long after they leave the military.*
>
> *Tommy said to me, "Where have you been Terry? I haven't seen you in a while."*

I gave him the very best excuse I could come up with. True, it's probably the lamest and most common mother of all excuses. I said, "Man! I have just been too busy to make it to the gym."

He looked at me and shook his head, and his reply has stuck with me throughout the years. Tommy said, "That's okay, if you forget to workout, don't worry, your body will soon remind you."

Life has a way of reminding us when the most important things are forgotten, especially when we begin to neglect our bodies. When we exercise, our bodies produce endorphins which aid in keeping us mentally and emotionally healthy.

It is said that a body in motion stays in motion, and it is also true that a body without motion gradually breaks down and can become a major limiting factor for a leader. Leaders must remember just how important it is to take care of their bodies and make a commitment to paying it the respect and attention it needs.

If we pay our bodies the attention they need, they will reward us, and if we forget about them, be sure they will find a way of reminding us about their importance.

Spiritual

For some of us it takes only one glance into the vastness of our sky to realize that we are a part of something much bigger than ourselves.

Teilhard de Chardin,[107] 18th century Jesuit priest and philosopher, taught, "*We are not human beings having a spiritual experience. We are spiritual beings having a human experience.*"

The greatest leaders of the past were very public about their spirituality. Take for example the famous words of Abraham Lincoln, "*I am profitably engaged in reading the Bible. Take all of this book upon reason that you can, and the balance by faith, and you will live and die a better man.*"[108]

Ronald Reagan once reminded our nation, "*If we ever forget that we're one nation under God, then we will be one nation gone under.*"[109]

John Wooden is arguably one of the best coaches of all time. During his life, he created a code to live by. His code was, "*Be true to yourself, help others, make each day your masterpiece, make friendship a fine art, drink deeply from good books - especially the Bible, build a shelter against a rainy day, give thanks for your blessings and pray for guidance every day.*"[110]

While this is just a very cursory overview of spirituality, my intention is to shine light on the importance of the spiritual component of a leader's core.

If the greatest leaders in history exercised their spirituality, we as Evolving Leaders should pay close attention to ours.

Purpose

Great leaders always have a Purpose at their core. Their purpose is what compels them to further their mission. A great leader's purpose is typically self-effacing and benefits others much more than it benefits the leader.

The size of one's purpose is irrelevant. What matters is that the leader understands they were put on this Earth for the benefit of others. Bertrand Russell, famed philosopher and atheist said, "*Unless you assume a God, the question of life's purpose is meaningless.*"[111]

The very minute we believe that we were put on this Earth for a purpose greater than ourselves, an entire world of opportunities opens up to us. We begin to see life as a mission instead of an obstacle. We begin to absorb life, instead of running from it.

People are attracted to leaders with purpose, because they see goodness at work in the leader's actions. Leaders with purpose wake up every day, and instead of feeling dread, they are full of life and love. They realize their destiny is tied to the lives of those they are leading.

As Evolving Leaders, we can use a litmus test for our purpose by asking ourselves the following questions.

- Are my daily actions focused on serving myself or others?

- Are my actions bringing me glory or are they glorifying something much bigger than myself?

Creativity

Creativity lies at the very core of every human being. Great leaders understand its importance and how to harness its power.

Each of us has a unique creative ability that only we were given that differentiates ourselves from all others. When we lay down the fear of what others might think, we can harness our creativity and become the leaders we are meant to be.

Most people default to saying, *"Well I am just not a creative type."* They fail to realize their very existence is an act of creativity. If we will believe in ourselves, from our heart and minds will flow a great creative source of goodness we can offer to others. Our creative offering is meant to enrich the lives of others, but we must first believe in our own creative powers before we can use them.

Pablo Picasso, one of the great creative geniuses of the past said, *"Inspiration exists, but it has to find you working."*[112]

What most people fail to realize is that just like architecture, breakthrough theory, or scholarly literature, creativity takes an incredible amount of discipline to bring to life.

A great writer was once asked, *"Do you wait for inspiration to hit you before you decided to write?"* His reply was, *"Yes but it happens to hit me every morning at nine in themorning when I am scheduled to sit down at my writing table.*"113

Leaders – you were created, and you are creative.

Harness the uniqueness that only you have, and use it to build your own work of art; create a new leadership model, write a book, or build a new relationship. Self-expression has a longing to be shared with others, and it is our job to let it out to help inspire others. Albert Einstein said it best, *"Those who have the privilege to know, have the duty to act, and in that action are the seeds of new knowledge."*114

Now that you know that at your very core is a creative power source, it is time to act.

Begin today exercising your creative muscles. Realize you are a created being, and creativity is in your very nature.

Once you understand what is at the core of your being, you can then go on and begin to use yourself efficiently to maximize your impact in life.

20. Priorities and Delegation

"If you chase two rabbits, you'll catch none." [115]
Russian Proverb

Time is the great equalizer for all leaders.

We as leaders can only do a few things really well, and it is incumbent upon us to decide what we will do with our limited time. Leaders need to constantly ask themselves the question, *"What are the few critical things that I can do really well?"*

Since time is one of the few things we can lose and never get back, it's imperative for us to prioritize. It is true that, we can never lose the past, we can never lose the future, but we can always lose today if we are not intentional about its importance.

Leaders should be protective of and strategic in the use of their time, so they can accomplish that which is most important.

Have you ever known an idea person? They have hundreds of ideas, and they want to chase every one of them. It seems that every week they have switched to their new idea or venture and it is the hottest thing. A few weeks later they are off to the next hot idea. These idea people never seem to get traction with anything, because they are chasing everything. There is nothing innately wrong with these people, they just become distracted by every shiny object that flashes in front of them.

Marketers love these people, because they will buy anything that has a call to action, and smells of success. These types of unfocused individuals often chase their tail, round and round, most of their life until they are exhausted. They metaphorically throw in the towel, because they cannot decide on which color towel they want to hang on to.

Andy Stanley often talks about the importance of delegation and priorities. He has created one of the largest churches in America. I reference volunteer organizations such as churches when I am researching because of the leadership that must be exhibited to build them. Andy recalls a lesson in delegation from one of his mentors, Dr. Howard Hendricks shared, *"If anything has kept me on track all these years, it's being skewered to this principle of central focus. There are many things I can do, but I have to narrow it down to the one thing I must do. The secret of concentration is elimination."*[116]

We are often confused between busyness and effectiveness. It is wrong to think that *"being busy"* is the same as *"making progress."* Doing more does not equal accomplishing more. Peter Drucker reminds us that doing the *things right* is much different from doing the *right things*. Drucker explains in his seminal writing *"The Effective Executive,"* that leaders *"Force themselves to set priorities and stay with their priority decisions. They know that they have no choice but to do first things first – and second things not at all."*[117]

Drucker was nicknamed *"The Father of Management"* because of his prolific contributions to the way businesses are built and are best managed.

Leaders build their foundation on personal management. If leaders cannot lead nor manage themselves, they cannot lead others effectively.

Leaders must realize they often have to give up good so that they can grab hold of what is best. They follow their gut and access all of their mental faculty to solidify their focus on the few critical things they believe will make the biggest difference in their organizations.

Leaders should focus on the few things that will yield the greatest results. The great entrepreneur, Andrew Carnegie, spent time in various industries amassing the largest wealth the nation had ever seen. He did this through concentration. He taught to concentrate your energies, your thoughts and your capital. *"The wise man puts all his eggs in one basket and watches the basket."*[118]

The enemy of leadership and any great accomplishment is distraction. Today we are bombarded with infomercials, spam mail, social media clickbait, pop-up banners in addition to all the traditional distractors such as billboards and dancing sign holders. The sole purpose of the great nemesis named "*Distraction*" is to keep us from making progress.

Leaders must become specialists. They must know how to block out the noise of life, so they can accomplish what is most important. In this new information era, **leaders now differentiate themselves by exercising their ability to concentrate their energy on a set of priorities**.

One of the great tools I use to set priorities comes from a story about the great manufacturing executive Charles Schwab. I have used this method of prioritization ever since I learned about it, and it works!

Charles M. Schwab,[119] president of Bethlehem Steel, became one of the richest men in history and greatest industrial leaders by adopting the Ivy Lee Method of prioritizing his days. Ivy Lee was a management consultant that Schwab hired to help him and his company come up with a more efficient way of doing things.

> *After a thorough evaluation of Schwab's operations, Ivy Lee explained that he had a way that would help increase the efficiency of Bethlehem Steel exponentially. Schwab, eager to learn, called a*

meeting of his top leaders to learn the new method of doing things. Ivy's instructions were simple:

1. *At the end of each day sit down and list your top six priorities for the next day.*

2. *Do not write more than six priorities for each day.*

3. *Rank order the priories 1 – 6. One being the most important.*

4. *Come in the next day and focus all your efforts on your priorities in order.*

5. *At the end of the day, repeat the process.*

Ivy told Schwab, "Do this every workday....after you're convinced of the value of this system, have your people try it out....and then send me a check for whatever you think the idea is worth."

After a few weeks of trying the new method, Schwab sent Ivy a check for $25,000, ($417,000 in today's dollars) with a message that explained Ivy's method was the best efficiency tool he has ever used.

Bethlehem Steel, under Schwab's leadership, went on to become the largest shipbuilder, and second largest steel manufacturer in the world.

"Simplicity is the ultimate sophistication."
William Gaddis[120]

There is incredible power in prioritization.

Leaders are often pulled in different directions because of the dynamics of business, and they can sometimes get through an entire day – only to look back on the day and wonder what they accomplished. Leaders often feel like firefighters who spend their time dowsing mini-fires created throughout their team or organization. This is a very reactive way for leaders to spend their time.

Instead, they should be proactive with their time and priorities by creating a non-negotiable list of what they must accomplish in a day. If the Ivy method is too simple for you, come up with your own method. But make sure that when you are done with your day, you can look back at what you have accomplished, and see some fruits of your labor surrounding what is most important.

When leaders look at prioritizing, they should always keep their people top of mind. Our priorities as leaders must include knowledge and authority transfer to others. As a leader, one of the greatest things we can do is help develop more leaders.

By keeping our people as top priorities, we do two things. First, we pay attention to the most important pieces of an organization: our people. And we also create a path for delegation. When we design our priorities to include developing our people, our people will be ready when there is a need to delegate.

Leaders will never be able to accomplish their priorities without delegation because problems naturally flow towards the person with the most authority. Great leaders develop other leaders and constantly push decision making authority to them – this is the essence of delegation. If we fail to develop leaders who are prepared to make decisions, we become choked out by the minutiae of daily operations.

The Ritz-Carlton name is synonymous with excellence. The Ritz-Carlton has published its philosophy which is called "Gold Standards."[121] Within the philosophy is a motto which says, "*We are Ladies and Gentlemen serving Ladies and Gentlemen.*"

This motto exemplifies the anticipatory service provided by all staff members. It goes on to state, "*At the Ritz-Carlton, our Ladies and Gentlemen are the most important resource in our service commitment to our guests.*"

The Ritz-Carlton is one of the best examples of an organization that pushes authority down to all employees a.k.a. "*Ladies and Gentlemen.*" Ritz-Carlton's President, Simon Cooper, explains how the organization goes about empowering their team – "*We entrust every single Ritz-Carlton staff member, without approval from their general manager, to spend up to $2,000 on a guest. And that's not per year. It's per incident.*" Hence the name "Gold Standards."[122]

The way to empower our people is to give them control over valuable resources and let them make decisions. Trust and empowerment are inextricably linked to great leadership.

The more authority we give away, the stronger others become. In turn, we as leaders and our teams become stronger, and more capable of serving others. When we empower others, they can make full use of their talents and experience.

Gary Keller, co-founder of the largest real estate franchise in the world, uses what he calls *"clarifying questions"* to help him prioritize his day. He asks himself, *"What's the one thing I can do such that by doing it everything else will be easier or unnecessary?"*[123]

Your answer to this question should help you prioritize and minimize your tasks simultaneously. I know from personal experience that Gary Keller's company, Keller Williams, spends a great deal of money on people development, so they can empower their people to make decisions.

Let me give you a suggestion when using the clarifying question that Gary suggests in your daily routine. Think about your people, then modify the question and ask *"What is the one thing that I can do to help my people become more capable and confident in their leadership abilities?"*

When you come up with the answer, act on it consistently. Over time you will see your people begin to flourish and take on a new sense of worth because of all they are able to accomplish as leaders.

As leaders we must understand there is a fundamental human desire at the core of every human being. Humans were designed to work and accomplish things. Through working, we bring value into our lives and the lives of others, and in turn, we feel valuable. We, as humans, are utilitarian – meaning we are designed for utility. Because of this fundamental nature, we have an innate desire to be fulfilled through progress. If we are not progressing in a meaningful way, we begin to feel like we are less valuable or in other terms *"worth - less."* As leaders, we have to be aware of this and do our best to combat it.

Stephen Covey helps uncover the importance of delegation when he shares, *"We accomplish all that we do through delegation–either to time or to other people. When we delegate to time, we think efficiency. If we delegate to other people, we think effectiveness."*[124]

Covey goes on to tell a great story of delegation:

> *Delegation means growth, both for individuals and for organizations. The late J.C. Penney was quoted as saying that the wisest decision he ever made was to "let go" after realizing that he couldn't do it all by himself any longer. That decision, made long ago, enabled the development and growth of hundreds of stores and thousands of people.*

A pivotal point in a leader's personal growth is the moment they realize they cannot do everything on their own. They have a choice to make at this point. They can either continue trying to do everything themselves, which will lead to burnout, or they can discover the critical power of delegation, which will take the leader and their people to the next level of achievement. Andy Stanley says this of delegation, "*When a leader can't find someone to hand things off to it is time for him to look in the mirror. We must never forget that the people who follow us are exactly where we have led them. If there is not one to whom we can delegate, it is our own fault.*"[125]

There is a brilliant fable by the Greek storyteller Aesop that teaches us the importance of priorities and delegation.

> *The story goes like this, "There was a man who found a goose that one day laid a golden egg. Upon discovering the egg, the man had the egg tested to determine if it was real gold, and much to his surprise it was. The man guarded the goose and continued to harvest the golden eggs as soon as they were laid.*
>
> *This man became rich and famous and his lifestyle became more and more elaborate. Soon the man needed more golden eggs to keep up with the demands of his lifestyle. The pressure of his greed mounted, so in order to harvest more eggs, one day the man decided to cut the goose open in hopes of finding more golden eggs. In cutting the goose open he ended its life, and in doing so ended his personal success and future. The man's life quickly crumbled due to his need to have more!*"[126]

The moral of this short story is simple but profound. If we do not protect our greatest asset, ourselves, we will end up ruining our only way of contributing to life.

On the other hand, if we embrace priorities and delegation, we will always know what must get done, and be able to determine who is best for getting it done, while simultaneously preserving ourselves and empowering others.

Knowing how to prioritize and delegate is essential to the evolution of a leader. If we believe this, we will benefit ourselves and others greatly. If we decide to do it all ourselves, we may become the goose in Aesop's fable.

Finally, when we operate in our priorities, we must be able to say "*No.*" Saying "*No*" is hard for leaders, because we want to set an example, be supportive and help others. While these are all great things to desire, the fact is, we cannot make everyone happy, and if we think we can, we are fooling ourselves.

As a leader progresses in life, the requests for their attention and time mount. There comes a point where if we are not careful, we will sacrifice what is most important to appease others. That is a fatal leadership trap. Knowing that we as leaders must say "*No*" is fundamental to our evolution because it protects our ability to prioritize and accomplish what is most critical to the mission. Saying "No" to the things that are not mission critical will protect one of our greatest assets – our time.

21. Goals and Commitments

"Goals and commitments are the catalysts and promises of future improvement."
Terry Weaver

Commitments are the glue that hold relationships together.

We make progress in life by making commitments and then maintaining the integrity to keep them. We also improve ourselves by setting goals and doing our best to achieve them.

Every year I set goals, and every year I fall short of accomplishing all of them, but I also accomplish some of them. But without goals, we have no measuring stick to evaluate ourselves. Evolving leaders should have personal and professional goals that will not only challenge them, but also help hold them accountable. Leaders should always be stretching themselves in life.

One of the best ways to stretch ourselves is by setting at least one big goal each year. In the book *Built to Last,*[127] the acronym "BHAG" (Big Hairy Audacious Goal) was coined. Having a personal and professional BHAG will keep us developing and moving forward.

If we as leaders do not evolve and move forward, the world will pass us by, because it is constantly changing and evolving.

All leaders should set personal goals. If it were not for a personal goal that I set to write this book, you would not be reading it now.

Our personal goals should help drive our professional goals. Once leaders have established their goals, they can then ask others to also establish goals and they can influence them to accomplish them. Just imagine if an entire team or organization set stretch goals, both personally and professionally. This would make a tremendous impact for everyone. It would benefit the individual contributor, the customers, and the organization itself. But if we as leaders do not have goals, we do not have the right to ask or influence others about their goals.

Let me give you a practical example – travel with me for a minute. Precisely twenty-four days ago I set a goal to write this book to share ideas about how to evolve as a leader. The next day I began writing. I then publicly shared my goal to write a book. Then I began asking my friends what their goals for the New Year were. Many of them responded with goals like: write a book, start a new venture, give a speech in front of a huge crowd, etc.… Since making the commitment to write this book, 19,538 words have been typed. This would never have happened if I did not make the commitment to myself and then publicly proclaim the goal. I can now help hold my friends accountable to their goals, because I am holding myself accountable to mine.

We should do our very best to keep both goals and commitments, but I want to differentiate the way a leader sees and treats both of these promises.

If we set goals and keep them to ourselves and then decide not to achieve those goals, we only harm ourselves. We rob ourselves of the achievement that we promised to give ourselves in the future. But when we make a commitment to others either specifically, or by implication, and decide not to follow through, we rob them and ourselves of the outcome of the commitment. If we make a habit of making commitments and not following through, we begin to chip away at our personal integrity.

It is important to understand that any kind of commitment should be kept, even if you have to fight for it, especially when it involves others. It is also important to understand that if we cannot make and keep commitments to ourselves, it is almost impossible to do it with others. Leadership begins with keeping the commitments we make to ourselves.

Keeping commitments builds strong relationships. Building a relationship is like building a brick house. Each brick laid on the foundation represents a promise made and kept. Over time we are able to strengthen the house if we continue to make and keep promises. The foundation of our relationships continue to grow stronger as we lay a good foundation and build on it. The opposite is also true, if instead we do not follow through on our word, we begin to remove bricks and the very foundation of our relationships become weak. Over time if we remove enough of them, the house is no longer suitable to dwell in.

Relationships break down just like structures that do not have enough support. The integrity of our relationships is what makes them thrive, and a lack of integrity is what chips away at them.

As leaders, we are only as good as our words and the action that follows them. **The old saying "*Your word is your bond*" is as relevant as ever.**

As leaders we must be able make and keep commitments in order to build strong relationships.

22. Leaders and their Power

*"There are only three kinds of people – those
who are immovable, those who are movable,
and those who move them!"*
Li Hung[128]

One of the greatest powers of a leader is their ability to
influence others.

Leaders have disproportionate power to others. Leaders
have the power to mark the lives of others for good or bad. A
wise friend of mine reminds me that, *"As leaders our
influence is never neutral, it is either building someone up or
tearing them down."[129]*

There are things that leaders have said to me in my past
that I will never forget. Because leaders hold power, they
must be especially careful when being critical of others even
if the intention is meant to be constructive. My beautiful and
intelligent wife often reminds our family that our words have

power in them – and she is right. When emotions flare, we tend to get very loose with what we say. And if we speak them when we are angry, we are likely to regret what we have said.

Some of the greatest leaders of history were born with an innate ability to lead. While I believe that much of leadership can be learned, the leader who was born with a gift of leadership has an advantage, and a head start. Having the gift of leadership implies that it should be treated with respect. As one notable teacher reminds us,

> "If you have been blessed with the gift of leadership, remember it is just that – a gift. But owning the gift and operating the gift responsibly are two different things. One requires nothing on your part. The other requires a lifetime of learning....recognizing your giftedness is unavoidable. But taking the time to develop the maturity to handle it responsibly requires initiative and discipline."[130]

When a leader realizes their power, they need to understand the difference between owning the gift of leadership and being a good steward of it. A leader becomes a good steward when they share the gifts they have been given with others in a responsible way.

One sure way to become a good steward of our leadership is through positive affirmations. They are very powerful for ourselves, but they are even more powerful for others.

Affirming others, is a part of our responsibility as leaders. We should be building others up through our words and actions. Speaking a positive affirmation into someone's life can leave a powerful mark on their life. When we affirm someone, it does something for their spirit – it is like giving them an emotional and intellectual recharge. The amazing thing about the power of affirmation is that it costs leaders very little, but the value of it to the receiver is monumental. Remember, people need to hear that they are valuable in life, and we as leaders can fulfill the need by affirming who they are.

> "Every man I meet is my superior in some way.
> In that, I learn of him."
> Emerson [131]

If we maintain the mindset that others are superior to us in some way, we can find their gift or specialty and affirm them in it.

I will never forget the day one of my college professors spoke a word of encouragement into my life. It will forever impact the way I see myself. After giving a talk in front of my fellow students, he looked at me and said, "*Terry, you have a very fatherly voice and a great heart, don't stop using them to speak into the lives of others.*"[132]

Until he said these words, I had a negative perception about the way I sounded when I spoke that could have limited my public speaking. But that day, my professor gave me a positive affirmation, and it fundamentally changed the way I think about myself. Leaders must know that genuine and humble affirmation is one of the greatest gifts we can give to another human being.

A leader who shares their power with others, will gain a reputation as one who is trusted and worth following.

Great leaders have a way of sharing their strength with others by helping them find hope. Hope, by definition, is believing in something that cannot be seen.

Until my professor told me that I had an impactful way of communication, I was blind to it. But because of the power of his leadership, I now believe something very different.

Leaders hold the ability to give hope to people who may never realize their true worth. This is the significant power of any leader. It is the reason that leadership should be recognized and handled with great care. It is an important responsibility.

Leaders have the power to build up and give hope to those around them through encouragement and positive affirmations. But leaders also have the ability to destroy and tear down the lives, and dreams of the people whom they lead. We get to choose how we will use our power!

23. The Leader's Tension

"The tension between who we are and who we want to be is oftentimes our future self, demanding us to flourish."
Terry Weaver

Where there's not progress, there's not growth. If there is not growth, a piece of the leader's life is missing. Environments void of change are eventually void of life.

So leaders find themselves in the precarious and often career-jeopardizing position of being the one to draw attention to the need for change.

Consequently, courage is a nonnegotiable quality for the next generation leader.[133]

It never fails that every few months I begin to ask myself the same questions.

- Am I on the right path?

- Should I make a change?

- Am I living life to its fullest?

> *"It seems my restless tension never goes away, and I feel that change is inevitable. I question where this restlessness comes from. I sometimes wonder if others wrestle with the same tension to reinvent, or to change course. I often wonder if this tension stems from some kind of unhappiness or if it is a healthy desire to continue to flourish as a human. I fear that always questioning whether I am making enough progress keeps me from enjoying the present. Thinking deeply about this constant struggle has helped me look for meaning in it, and to find answers to why the struggle exists."*

As leaders, we can get stuck in a gray area where it seems there is no clear solution or direction in life. The reality that we are free to make choices in life can bind us to the vastness of choice, and into endless uncertainty. Because of this, I find that it can sometimes be helpful to reform our thinking into black and white logic driven decision making. This can help us choose one direction over the other.

We can ask ourselves leading questions that have a clear dichotomy between two extremes. For example, when looking at our future trajectory or lack thereof – would we choose between inertia or change? Or put more simply, we can ask, *"In my current state, would I choose to stay the same or continue to push myself to become better?"*

I often remind myself of the fact, *"The only way to coast is downhill."*[134]

The truth is, there really is no such thing as staying the same. Physics and biology state that everything is either growing, or being broken down, or some combination of both. Kevin Kelly, in his book *The Inevitable*, remarks, *"Everything without exception, requires additional energy and order to maintain itself. I know this in the abstract as the famous second law of thermodynamics, which states that everything is falling apart slowly"*....even human beings (my note)!"[135]

Kevin goes on to explain that even something as static as computer code is gradually falling apart, and if it is not maintained, the code itself will eventually become useless.

There is a natural tension between who we are today and who we will be tomorrow, but we get to choose what to do with that tension. It is neither good nor bad, but we have to address it; otherwise it will address us.

This also means that even staying the same requires some level of struggle and will produce a tension in our state of being. Remember the saying, *"A body in motion stays in motion?"*[136]

Have you noticed it takes significant effort to reach a notable level of athleticism, but it takes almost nothing to lose that level of athleticism? It really is unfair. Let's take for example a mile-long run. For the average individual, it takes weeks and sometimes months to become comfortable with running a mile, but it is also true that if that same person decides to not run a mile for two weeks, the ability run a mile is quickly diminished. This is one example of the truth that everything is falling apart, or diminishing over time.

While attending a leadership conference, I heard John Maxwell speak. Maxwell is one of the most prolific authors on the subjects of leadership and personal growth. He shared that as leaders, "*Our Big Picture should keep getting bigger.*"[137]

This reminds me that we cannot grow without change. If we want to get better, we must see the tension between who we are today and who we desire to become as a valuable opportunity to grow, and become better for ourselves and also for others.

Abraham Lincoln quipped, "*God must love the common man, He made so many of them.*"[138]

As leaders, we should be afraid of what we might not accomplish if we decide to allow ourselves to stay the same. In an interview with Steve McKinney, *a.k.a* "*The Legend,*" who spent ten years as an NFL offensive lineman with the Texans, Seahawks and Colts, he shared that there are a few quotes he has posted on his bathroom mirror. They remind him to keep seeking improvement. One of them is, "*I have no interest in being average*" and the other, "*Good is the Enemy of Great.*"[139]

Steve shared that his favorite NFL Coach, Howard Mudd, constantly reminded him, "*Whether you think you can, or you think you can't, you are right.*"[140] In Steve's post NFL career, he's become an entrepreneur in the franchising business.

Steve made a decision to become a McDonald's franchise owner only to be denied when he submitted his application. After being rejected, he had all kinds of negative thoughts ranging from, "*Don't these guys know who I am?*" to "*Maybe I am not qualified.*"

Steve went on to share that throughout his life, when he made a decision to accomplish something, he never let anything stop him. As a child, after watching his favorite college football team, the Aggies, play a hard-fought game, he made a decision that someday he would win a spot on the team. A similar decision was made when he was a starting football player with the Aggies – he made the decision that someday he would play football for the NFL. Steve shared that once he made a decision to achieve something, it was then time to put in the dogged work to make the decision a reality.

After his NFL career, as fate or luck would have it, Steve randomly met someone who had strong ties with the McDonald's Corporation. Steve reapplied to become a McDonald's franchisee. Steve's fierce determination led him to get his first franchise. He now owns ten franchises and his

Big Picture keeps getting bigger. Steve now has a goal to own thirty franchises in twenty years. The tension between who Steve is as a leader today and the leader he wants to be in the future pulls the best out of him. He continues to believe in the fact, *"Whether you think you can, or you think you can't, you are right."*

This point about the tension pulling on leaders to become more than they are today should not cause anxiety. But instead, it should help leaders become comfortable with being uncomfortable.

This knowledge can help leaders prepare expectations about what the future holds. The tension and the desire to become better is okay.

Everyone is faced with choices in life to either grow, maintain, or decline. Recognizing this tension in our lives can be either sobering or liberating, but for leaders it should be the latter.

24. Leaders Show Themselves

"Until a leader can show themselves, faults,
failings, triumphs and all, they will remain just a
shadow of their true capability."
Terry Weaver

Leaders are bold enough to put themselves out front.

This is the fundamental difference between leaders and all others. There is something inside them that propels them to get out in front of the crowd. But there is major fear one has to overcome to be able to do this. There is fear of rejection, fear of what others will think, and fear of making a mistake. But if we can muster the courage to step out, we will begin to show our true selves. Our uniqueness is what sets us apart. If we decide to live in any form of fear, we are making a conscious decision to keep our uniqueness, the very thing that sets us apart, hidden from the world.

Leaders show their ink!

Dr. Todd Dewett taught me this. While speaking to a crowd of people he said, *"We can't be afraid to show our true colors."*[141] Todd Dewett is a leading author on topics of leadership and authenticity. His writing and public speaking have helped thousands of leaders break out of their fears.

I was one of them. I was afraid of what others might think about me. I was ready to break out of fear, so in preparation for Dr. Dewett's keynote, I decided I was going to show my true colors.

The morning of Dr. Dewett's talk, I was working out with a friend of mine who is tattooed from his head to the bottom of his butt cheeks[5]. I asked my friend to join me for the talk that Todd was going to give that night. I said to him, "We have this leadership guru coming to speak for us. He's all tatted up and the title of his keynote is "Show Your Ink." You should come and listen and show off some of your ink."

Right after I invited my friend, I began to think to myself, "How should I show my ink and be authentic?"

At the time I had a few tattoos myself, but I always kept them hidden from fear of what others might think. But it caused a problem for me. I had organized a talk about authenticity and talked an expert into coming out and speaking for us. I had also invited my friend and told him to be authentic

---

[5] I have knowledge of my friend's tattoo details, buns and all, because he posted a picture of his fresh ink the day he completed it.

and show off some of his unique tattoos. But what was I prepared to do?

I began to question my own integrity. I asked myself "How can I embrace authenticity without being authentic myself?"

I noticed a difference in what I was asking other to do and what I was willing to do myself, so I decided to show my ink that night.

When I arrived the night of Dr. Dewett's talk, I had a pinstriped suit on. I greeted all the guests as they arrived. After most of the guests had arrived, my friend showed up. He had a white polo on that showed of his elaborate ink.

The time was perfect, so I peeled of my suit jacket.....

At home about an hour before I had taken a perfectly dry-cleaned shirt that I planned on wearing and chopped off the sleeves at the shoulder. Then I put the shirt on, tied my tie as usual, and put my suit jacket on like normal.

When I pulled off my jacket, people saw that I was not like the others who were sporting usual business attire. I had a suit, a tie, and a really nice collared shirt on that was missing its sleeves. I was embracing my ink and being courageous enough to show it.

There was nothing heroic about it, but for some reason, that night was a bit of a turning point for me. People were drawn to me because of my unique markings – the tattoos I showed on both of my shoulders. They wanted pictures with the sleeveless host who was showing his ink.

Ever since that day, I have tried to be unafraid of showing my ink. There were three people in the room who showed their ink: Dr. Todd Dewett, my friend, and me. It was freeing! It was a small act of courage that had a ripple effect in my life. That night I showed up unafraid and showed who I was. I joined the minority of liberated individuals who are willing to "Show Their Ink."

Just to clarify, showing yourself requires zero ink, but it does require some courage. It starts with showing how you are unique in a sea of homogenous people. Great leaders demonstrate their uniqueness and courage to stand out front and set a path for others to follow.

This starts with the leader looking inside themselves and saying, *"It is okay to be you...faults and all."*

Then it takes some inner courage to expose *"Who we are to the world."*

You are unique for a reason…. You're a specialist when embracing the uniquely you. When you show yourself – strengths, weaknesses, habits, hang-ups and all, then say to the world, *"World here I am, like it or not, I am moving forward, and I am taking people with me,"* others will be emboldened by your courage, and they will follow you.

One of my favorite authors on the topic of authenticity is Brené Brown.[142] Her writing on leadership, vulnerability, and courage is eye-opening. In her book *"Dare to Lead,"* she talks about having *"The heart of daring leadership."* She identifies the four skill sets needed to have the courage to lead. One of the skill sets is what she calls *"Rumbling with Vulnerability."* This really boils down to showing your weakness, struggles, and faults as a human, and having the courage to work through them. Brené explains,

> "The foundational skill of courage-building is the willingness and ability to rumble with vulnerability. Without this core skill the other three skill sets are impossible to put into practice….our ability to be daring leaders will never be greater than our capacity for vulnerability. Once we start to build vulnerability skills, we can start to develop the other skill sets."[143]

Showing our authentic self – strengths, flaws, tattoos, beliefs, and limitations will help us lay the foundation to build additional leadership skills. We are just a shadow of what we could be as a leader if we aren't true to ourselves, and about ourselves.

The alternative to being *courageously you* is living a life of untapped potential and regret. Bronnie Ware, a palliative care nurse, has experienced many people dying first hand and has done extensive writing on the top five regrets of the human life. Bronnie asked many people at the end of their life the question, *"What is your biggest regret?"[144]*

The most common response to the question is sobering and revealing – *"I wish I'd had the courage to live a life true to myself, not the life others expected of me."*

Why do most people live in fear of being uniquely themselves, and instead live their life to appease others?

Everyone reading this book should take a minute right now to ask themselves the same question that Bronnie asked those she interviewed at the end of their life. *"What is your biggest regret of your life?"*

_____

_____

_____

_____

And now that you have the answer, you must do something about that regret! Remember, without change, there can be no growth.

Living a *"life of voyeurism"* is the common route that most people take when they don't want to deal with this. It is too easy to plug into being someone else. It is too easy to sit back on the couch and pretend you are living a life of excitement by watching it on the flat screen. We become masters of comfortability, and we ask ourselves, *"Why should I do the 100 mile challenge run, when I can watch it on television and avoid all the pain it takes to train for and accomplish it."*

Instead of actually living, these people opt to sit back and vicariously watch those out front facing their fears. This is very safe way to live…or is it? How can we call it *"living,"* if it ultimately leads to regret?

Today it is easy to throw on the virtual reality headset and instantly become the bold version of you. But in reality, it takes courage to step out the front door and face our biggest fears. The bigger the fear, the more likely we are to back down and retreat. But instead we should charge toward our fears and conquer them one-by-one!

This is a call to action for each and every one of us….write down the one thing that you are terrified of – that you know you would regret at the end of your life if you did not now attempt it. Do not pass this one over.

Write it down now, and make a commitment to yourself that you are going to chase after this dragon and slay it.

_____

_____

_____

_____

By being *courageously you,* you'll seek out and find the power that you need to face your fears. You will begin to build on your courage day-by-day. Your confidence will grow slowly but surely, and your future regrets will begin to disappear.

You will become the person you are meant to be – uniquely you, the person you were intended to be. If you will commit to a bold charge towards you dreams, they will begin to come true today.

25. Leaders and Hard Work

"Hard work is what lies in the valley between mediocrity and extraordinary."
Terry Weaver

In an interview with Steven Hummer, United States Marine Corps Lieutenant General (3 Star General) Ret., I asked about key principles of leadership.[145] General Hummer retired after 41 years of service. He deployed over 20 times during his career. He has some serious experience leading thousands of leaders.

In our interview he passionately shared, while hammering his fist on the table, *"Leadership is 24/7 you can't go to work a 9am and punch out at 5pm and say, 'I am done with leadership for the day'. You are on all the time. You have to work harder for your people than they are working for you."*

Leaders who are afraid of hard work won't last. A strong work ethic is essential to becoming any kind of leader.

People are always watching and evaluating their leader, and if they see someone who is averse to hard work, they quickly write them off as *"Not Committed."*

Aside from the courage that it takes to step out and lead, it takes a tremendous amount of determination to do anything significant. Most people are dying while searching the book *"The Four Easy Steps to Success."* They search for a lifetime only to find out that they might as well invest in snake oil. Mark my words, the words *"Easy"* and *"Leadership"* do not belong together. These words won't live together for any sustained amount of time. If you want to lead, get ready for hard work – period!

Will Smith[146] is a leader of human performance. He uses his performance in music, television and movies. Will states that there is a big difference between talent and skill.

Talent is what we are born with; everyone gets talent. He says that skill is much different and explains that *"skill is only developed by hours and hours and hours of beating on your craft."*[147] Will Smith believes that greatness is inside all of us. He shared his thoughts on greatness in an interview with Charlie Rose – *"Greatness is not this wonderful esoteric elusive godlike feature that only the special among us will ever taste, it is something that truly exists in all of us."*[148]

Smith went on to explain that for one to be great they must be willing to say – *"This is what I believe, and I am willing to die for it."*[149]

Will's work ethic is his secret weapon and is an example of what it takes to succeed as a leader in any industry. In another interview, Will shared, *"I have never really viewed myself as particularly talented. I've viewed myself as slightly above average in talent. And where I excel is ridiculous, sickening, work ethic. You know, while the other guy is sleeping? I am working. While the other guy's eatin'? I am working."*[150]

In another interview, Will explained the difference between him and his competition is simply work ethic. *"The only thing that I see that is distinctly different about me is I am not afraid to die on a treadmill....I will not be outworked, period."*[151]

This is the type of work ethic it takes to get out in front and lead and do extraordinary things. When people see this type of work ethic, they become inspired, and they want to follow the inspiration.

> *"At the center of bringing any dream into fruition is self-discipline."*
> Will Smith[152]

LeBron James echoes the same message. In an interview with Tim Ferriss,[153] LeBron shared some of the ways he has become the leader that he is today. LeBron talked about his work ethic. He shared that right after the season ends, he is immediately back on the court training for the next season. He is in the weight room doing strength training, and he is on the track doing sprints. He out trains his competition.

LeBron is one of the most durable basketball players in the NBA. He has played over 50,000 hours while most players last about 40,000 hours, and he credits the success to his training fueled by his work ethic.

LeBron noted in the interview that his trainer is famous for telling him to slow down: *"He consistently tells me, 'Hey, listen, man. You need to take a little bit more time off. We just went for nine and a half straight months.' And I'm like, 'No'."*

Like Will Smith, LeBron pushes the limits and credits his success to hard work. LeBron explains that he studies leaders, so he can lead his family, team and himself. LeBron shared, *"Leadership is not a one-day thing....leadership is consistent. And I believe having longevity in the space that I'm in, is because of consistency as well, not only on the floor but off the floor as well."*

Some of LeBron's favorite leaders to study from the past are Dr. Martin Luther King, Jr, and Muhammad Ali.

In a packed auditorium Dwayne Johnson, better known as *"The Rock,"* gave one of the most inspiring talks I have ever heard. He opened by saying, *"No one will outwork me; no one! I love and I respect you guys; but you....will never outwork me....you have to be the hardest workers in a room."*[154]

Dwayne Johnson made the Forbes list of the highest paid actors of all time in 2018. When he received the news, he tweeted the response,

"I don't have a Harvard MBA, but my business philosophy has been sharpened over time and thru failure. I have one boss I serve and connect with - the world and the people in it. I'm the dude who started w/ $7bucks. I'm awestruck ($124M) grateful & hungry."

Not only is Johnson a successful actor,[155] but he is also one of the most successful professional wrestlers of all time, an NCAA national football champion, a motivational speaker, and a partner with Under Armour® in a lucrative endorsement deal. More recently, NBC has partnered with Dwayne Johnson to co-produce a new TV series. When asked about his success, his answer always stays the same. Dwayne credits his success to putting in really hard work.

Will Smith, LeBron James, and Dwayne Johnson are all extremely hard workers and leaders in their respective fields. You might ask how these three characters landed in a leadership book and here is why.

They are leading millions of people, and combined, they are influencing billions of people around the globe. They inspire people to work hard and push their human limits. They all agree their success is largely due to their work ethic, and they have publicly stated that the formula to their success is not brains, it is not a big fat inheritance, but instead it is their work ethic that has taken them to the pinnacle of their respective industries.

26. Leaders and Their Fire

"Deep inside of leaders there is a fire. We must continually stoke that fire, so that we have the fuel to charge forward. People will be drawn to your fire if it is bright."

Terry Weaver

Have you ever spent time around a leader who was just *"lukewarm?"* Think of someone who was just barely fired up about life and all of its limitless possibilities.

This description almost seems like a paradox, doesn't it?

Let me give you an example of the type of person I am describing here. When we ask a lukewarm person, *"What makes you excited?"*

They will usually refer to the past and say something along these lines, *"Well, when I was in my early thirties, I had this great role, in this exciting environment and it was great because… (Insert legendary example here)."*

These are people who have kept themselves from creating their future and have decided to dwell on their past for significance. Somehow, for some reason, they have allowed their "*fire*" to burn out.

A leader's first priority must be themselves. Their job is to identify what is burning inside of them. This is the one thing that has caused them to step into the arena of leading.

Most of the time, when we identify a leader who has done something significant with their life, it's because they have uncovered a passion that ignited something inside of them and then made a decision to share it with the world.

If you have identified your passion, then you also know the source of your "*fire*." Once that "*fire*" is identified, a leader must continue to find ways to fuel it and keep it burning hot!

> *"The most important conversations we will ever have, are the ones we have with ourselves."*
> David Goggins[156]

The arena in which we leaders have to compete in is brutal. We are beaten, chastised, criticized, then chewed up, and spit out. Sometimes all of this happens before we ever leave the house in the morning. After this happens a few times, doubt can be planted in a leader's mind. Self-doubt is what takes most leaders out. It is our job as leaders to fuel our thoughts and passions, so we can continue to share them with the world. This starts by combating all of the offensive attacks from both internal and external forces. One of the best ways to do this is by creating a positive message that we continue to replay in our own mind.

Back in 2014, I had convinced myself that I needed to take action on a project that was near and dear to my heart. The project that was brewing inside of me for a year or so, and it was what would later become a non–profit organization named the "VEL INSTITUTE."

I had this deep conviction that I needed to help veterans who had spent time serving our country, then transitioned back to civilian life and had somehow lost their way.

This passion was born from witnessing my friends deploy to a war zone and return. When they returned from a deployment, most times being a combat deployment, they came back different. Still to this day, I believe that when men and women deploy to a combat zone and then return to a normal environment, after-effects are inevitable.

In 2002, I was deployed to Iraq with the U.S. Marines. Throughout my deployment, I was in a constant state of fear of losing my life. Eventually I came to terms with the fact that there was a very real chance I would not return home. After I accepted the fact I might not leave the deployment alive, there was a shift in my mindset. I was able to relax a little bit....while in a war zone....

That is, until the sounds of war commenced. After the action began, my adrenaline kept me in a heightened state of awareness for much of the remaining deployment. All I needed to get me going was a nearby explosion, then the surge of adrenaline sent me into "fight of flight" mode.

After this happened a few times, real damage was done. I finished out my tour of Iraq without too much damage, or so I thought. It ended up taking me a very long period of pain to return to a so called normal life – but that story is for a different time.

I give this context to the readers to show how my *"fire"* was started. When I saw my friends, fellow servicemen and women struggling, I decided to do something about it. I did not start off knowing exactly what to do, I just knew I had to do something. When I made the decision to do something to help, I was almost instantly overwhelmed with self-doubt, and mental affliction. I remember many times after a long day at work, coming home at night to work on what turned into a passion project for me. Then after exhausting myself completely, I would take a bath to relax. (I love taking baths, it is where my best, and sometimes worst thinking takes place).

My thoughts would begin to run rampant.

"Who are you – to think you can do something to help others?"

"Sometimes you struggle to help yourself, how
could you possibly help others?"

"You grew up in a trailer park and almost didn't
make it through high school! What business do you
have starting an institute?"

"You had a broken childhood, a failed marriage,
you're barely making it out of your state of
depression....what makes you think you can be a
role model with that type of past?"

I could go on and on with this list of deep, dark, and insecure
questions that I asked myself. They plagued my mind –
these thoughts almost took me out. But instead of letting
them take over, I made a decision to stoke my fire with the
necessary fuel to keep it burning. The problem was too big
to ignore. I knew that self-loathing was only gonna get me
sent down the drain with the cold bath water.

Everyone is subject to these types of thoughts, especially
leaders who are taking risks to do something out of the
ordinary. You could've had a great childhood. You could
have never stepped foot in a war zone, and have had the
greatest education, but still the doubts of this world will hit
you hard. Everything that they bring with them will try to
sabotage you, to keep you from moving forward on your
dreams. The doubts that tend to take leaders out come in all

forms. They can stem from a divorce in your past, trouble with your best friend, or a critic on the internet.

Every doubt that causes us to question if we should continue, must be conquered. We as leaders have to keep our *"fire"* burning hot enough that it consumes the negative thoughts. Remember, our passion, and our "fire" as leaders are what keeps us moving towards significance.

There are many ways to stoke our *"fire,"* so I will just list a few that have worked for me and the leaders I have referenced in performing the research for this book.

- Prayer is my number one fuel source – it is what keeps my "fire" burning bright. Many great leaders have also used this source of fuel: e.g. Martin Luther King Jr., Abraham Lincoln, George Washington, and Maya Angelou. They all used prayer to stoke the *"fire"* that burned bright in them.

- Many leaders today meditate. I have never used traditional meditation, but I have close friends and mentors who do, and from what I understand, it is a great way to declutter your mind. It's a way of emptying the mind so it can be filled with the right thoughts. There are many different types of meditation, and I am sure I have not done it justice with this explanation. But at a minimum, I would like us to recognize it as a widely used source that leaders use to fuel their fire.

- Most of the leaders I studied in preparation for this book did some type of reflective journaling or writing. Andrew Carnegie notes, *"No man will leave a mark on history without putting pen to paper."*[157] Reflective writing helps us organize our thoughts and discard the ones that are not useful. I like to think of reflective writing or journaling as sending our thoughts to the cleaners to have the stains removed from them. By writing our ideas down, it gets them out of the massive collection of disparate ideas and helps us organize them in communicable form. One of my good friends and a mentor in my life, Bob Milner, keeps a *"Gratitude journal."*[158] He starts his day by recording five things he is thankful for. He says it helps keep that which is most important in his life top of mind. He says it also sets the tone for his day.

  I kept a *"gratitude journal"* for a year before I started my current routine that includes a form of *"reflective journaling."* Keeping a gratitude journal is powerful because it can be used as a tool to look back on and see just how much we have to be grateful for. If we need a little bit of *"fuel"* to add to our *"fire,"* we can simply open up our journal and look at everything we have stated that we are grateful for.

- Many people ascribe to the discipline of positive affirmations to start their day. A positive affirmation routine can be as simple as starting your day by saying something like, *"I am strong and courageous and I will make a difference with the thoughts and actions I have today."* We can repeat this statement or something similar daily to keep the flood of negative emotions and thoughts from holding us back from our purpose. Positive affirmations are used by many leaders today. I happen to practice a form of positive affirmations. I use scripture, proverbs, and quotes. I repeat them to myself daily to keep my doubts in check.

- Another way to *"fuel your fire"* is through <u>learning a new skill</u>. There are so many new ways to learn these days. We no longer have to travel to a brick and mortar structure to learn a new skill or educate ourselves. We have the ability to port the greatest instructors in the world right into the convenience of our home.

One of my favorite methods of learning is listening to podcasts. I have been listening to podcasts for years now, and they've become a great source of fuel for my fire. A leader can very quickly expand their breadth of knowledge by listening to podcasts.[6] Because of the proliferation and quality of podcasts today, we have access to some of the brightest minds such as: Elon Musk, Reid Hoffman, Tony Robbins, Peter Diamandis, Tim Ferriss and many, many more.

---

[6] I have provided a list of my favorite podcasts in Selected Reading & Resources at the back of this book.

- Another way to fuel our fire is by <u>pushing our physical capacity</u> to the next level. Our body is a gift that should be treated as such. Our body is the vehicle for our mind, communication, emotions, and actions. When we push ourselves physically either through some type of physical challenge or maintenance, we enable our mind, spirit, and emotions to run at optimal levels. Every leader will have a limiting factor, and that limiting factor is too often the leader's body.

  Leaders often rob Peter to pay Paul so severely that Peter ends up broke and Paul ends up dead. And unfortunately, it is true that we cannot prevent our bodies from becoming old, but we can do things to prevent them from feeling old. Leaders know how important it is to exercise because it is a source of fuel that keeps them strong.

- Lastly, I recommend this final way to fuel your fire because of how instrumental it has been in my leadership journey. One of the best ways to evolve as a leader is to assemble a small group of people; the best size is four to five men or women. This group will become your "<u>Personal Accountability Group</u>." These are individuals who you will ask to join you in a bi-weekly meeting with the sole purpose of helping *everyone* in the group get better.

  You will need to come up with a set of values that you all hold as highly important – these could be family, faith, fitness, marriage, or any other values you decide to form the group around. You will find that most high-level leaders have a personal accountability group to lean on in times of struggle. During your time with the group, you can hold the members accountable to the values the group was founded on. You will find that this group will become something you look forward to. It should become an anchor of strength for every member in the group.

I have had a personal group of four-five men who I meet with on a regular basis for over four years now. It is one of the best commitments I have ever made. This method of *"fueling my fire"* has been one of the best sources of *"fuel"* for my *"fire,"* and I plan to continue this for the rest of my life.

The reason I believe this method is so powerful is because it prevents the members of the group from retreating into isolation which is one of the most dangerous pitfalls of a leader. Isolation is a sure way to alienate yourself from the very thing that makes life and leadership so special which is relationships and the ability to help others.

I have written many suggestions in this section because the concept of leaders keeping a close watch on their fire and continuing to fuel it is imperative. If you fail to *"fuel your fire,"* mark my words, your passion will burn out!

If you want to start with one of these methods, do yourself a favor and take the last recommendation I listed and make it your first action item. Not only will you help yourself, but you will also help those who decide to join the group with you. There will be a ripple effect in their family, business, and relationships. There is an old, true proverb that stands true today:

As iron sharpens iron, so one man sharpens another.
Proverbs 27:17 (NIV)

Build your accountability group then begin to add additional sources of *"fuel"* to your *"fire."*

27. Leaders and Facts

"There is a thin line between fact and fantasy.
Leaders must continually pursue the truth."
Terry Weaver

There is a mandatory association between the leader and the truth otherwise known as *"Brutal Facts."*

Leaders must constantly try to uncover the truth, so they can make the best decisions. **The worst thing a leader can do is to ignore red flags that present themselves in any form.** Leaders have an obligation to seek out the truth and share it with their team. The best laid plans are never superior to new facts – the plans must be adjusted once the truth is realized.

Optimism never trumps reality.

Leaders need think of themselves like archaeologists, but instead of uncovering physical matter, they're working to uncover the truth in every matter. And just like archaeologists have many tools, leaders should understand that sometimes they will need to use different tools to uncover the truth. Sometimes they will need to use a metaphorical pick axe, and sometimes they will need to use a small brush to dust away the smallest of items covering the truth.

In the research for their best-selling book "*Good to Great,*"[159] Jim Collins and his team conceptualized what confronting the brutal facts should look like to a leader.

In an interview with Vice Admiral Jim Stockdale, a U.S. Navy Aviator and prisoner of war between the years of 1968 - 1973, Collins uncovered a great truth about leadership. Admiral Stockdale explained a psychology he developed that helped carry him through being tortured over twenty times when he was a prisoner of war during the Vietnam War. The mindset Stockdale developed helped Collins and his team formulate what they coined as "*The Stockdale Paradox.*"[160]

Admiral Stockdale explained that faith alone never guarantees that one will survive brutal situations, and it can sometimes become a fatal strategy. Stockdale explained that at times he actually beat himself with a stool, and cut his own wrists with a razor blade so his captors could not use him for manipulative propaganda to fool those back in the United States who were negotiating for his release. Then Captain Stockdale was the senior ranking prisoner of war, and his decision to become mentally tough helped give his fellow prisoners of war a sense of strength. Stockdale explained, "*I never doubted not only that I would get out, but also that I would prevail in the end and turn the experience into the defining event of my life, which, in retrospect, I would not trade.*"

He went on to explain that during his time as a POW he created a way to communicate to his fellow prisoners through an encoded language that helped them survive torture by allowing them to give certain amounts of uniform information to their captors. This was a strategy that allowed him and others to participate in their own survival instead of just maintaining blind hope that they would someday escape.

Stockdale also shared that he saw many of his fellow prisoners die over his eight years in the war camp. When Collins asked him what the difference was between those who died and those who made it out, he said that the optimists were the ones who didn't make it out. Stockdale clarified what he meant, "*The optimists. Oh, they were the ones who said, 'we're going to be out by Christmas.' And Christmas would come, and Christmas would go. Then they'd say, 'We're going to be out by Easter.' And Easter would come, and Easter would go. And then Thanksgiving, and then it would be Christmas again. And they died of a broken heart.*"[161]

Stockdale summarized the psychology of the survivors of the Hanoi Hilton war camp that helped them persevere until the day they were set free. "*This is a very important lesson. You must never confuse faith that you will prevail in the end – which you can never afford to lose – with the discipline to confront the most brutal facts of your current reality, whatever they might be.*"[162]

This is a powerful concept to solidify in our own psychology. It reminds us that, being optimistic that we will prevail as leaders is not enough. We must always confront the facts of our situation, so we can prepare, adjust, and create a winning strategy to prevail.

In addition, we must also maintain an optimistic point of view to "*fuel*" ourselves to be able to persevere through tumultuous times. But, eternal optimists oftentimes have "*blind spots*" that keep them from seeing that they are in the midst of a battle with reality. **Sometimes optimism blinds leaders and keeps them from seeing and confronting the brutal facts of life**.

Every leader must take inventory of their situation. They should constantly survey their conditions and assess the facts. There are countless failed leadership stories about those who put on blinders and used optimism to light their path only to find themselves crushed by the facts. This happened to Polaroid with the advent of digital photos and Blockbuster Video with the advent of Netflix. Public transportation is currently being reinvented by ride-sharing technology. Traditional retail stores are scrambling to combat their market share erosion that is happening because of e-commerce.

Leaders need not only pay attention to the brutal facts of the business environment, but they should also apply the "*Stockdale Paradox*" to their personal lives. We must constantly assess the facts in our relationships while maintaining optimism. Many leaders have toppled, because they optimistically believed their personal lives could weather a storm as long as they were putting enough work in at the office while just providing for their families. A fractured personal relationship can cause significant collateral damage in another area of a leader's life. It's all tied together.

The evolving leader should maintain an inside-out approach to life and leadership. It is important to understand that we will never be as healthy or productive in our leadership if we are not healthy and productive at our core.

To illustrate this idea, think of a beautiful apple. Have you ever bitten into a perfectly flawless apple only to find a dead cavern inside of it? When we find out that there is a dead portion in our perfect apple, everything changes… I don't know about you, but for me, the entire apple is ruined.

If we think of our life in this context, the inside must be as beautiful and healthy as the outside. There is no way to hide the brutal facts of our inner condition, so we must confront them, and deal with them. By continually doing core maintenance, a leader can ensure that their actions and motives are in alignment with their values and who they are even when no one is looking.

28. Leaders and Discipline

"Things which matter most must never be at the mercy of things which matter least."

Goethe[163]

If there is a recipe to becoming a leader, one of the key ingredients is discipline.

Discipline is a non-negotiable. It is the foundation of personal leadership, and without personal leadership, we cannot lead publicly. Put simply, if we cannot master leading ourselves, we have no business trying to lead others. When we look at leaders at the highest level, they all have one thing in common, they are disciplined. They follow a set routine. They have trained themselves to conform to a personal framework for their day that they have created. Remember, time is the great equalizer. If we do not handle it wisely, we may end up on our deathbeds with hearts and minds full of regrets.

Discipline is crucial for leaders because it allows them to focus on what is most important. It allows them to put first-things-first. Arguably, some of the most successful leaders of all time are Bill Gates and Warren Buffett. These men are often idolized, and made to look like they operate in a bubble. That is an illusion. You better believe they are running large dynamic organizations and that their leadership matters. In an interview, both Gates and Buffett were asked about the single largest contributor to their success. Their answers were identical – *"Focus."*[164]

Discipline allows the leader to block out the non-essentials, so they can become laser focused on the critical tasks. Discipline is more of a philosophy than it is an action. Great leaders usually believe they are most effective when they are *"firing on all cylinders."* So they pay the personal price to get the most out of their life hour-by-hour, and they do this through discipline. Discipline does not mean that as leaders we have to walk about like a cyborg with tunnel vision, but we do have to make a plan of action and stick to it if we want to lead successfully.

All it takes to prove out this concept of discipline is to take three of your current favorite leaders and Google their routines. You will find that a common denominator exists between leaders throughout the generations, without regard to industry, and that common denominator is a disciplined routine.

The greatest routines start with an early morning rising after some predefined sleep regimen. Leaders know they must focus on themselves first, so they can focus on others next. Many of them begin with a morning prayer or meditation. Other leaders begin their day with reflection or by stating what they are grateful for. Then many leaders find it helpful to review their day and confirm their priorities for their day. It is important to plan our days before we start them, otherwise we are at risk of being pulled away from what is important by something that is merely urgent.

Great leaders discipline themselves in all areas of their life. They discipline their mind, their body, and their soul by placing a priority on feeding each area appropriately, so they can function at the highest level.

> *For the last three years I have maintained a very disciplined routine. I wake up at 4:00 a.m. and grab my cup of coffee. I do my daily devotional reading from the Bible and then pray for roughly thirty minutes. After I am finished, I write, and then head off to the gym for at least an hour. By 9:00 a.m. I head off to work, and I already feel accomplished. I can go about the rest of the day knowing that if I chose to stop working, my day would be a huge success. I never do quit, but if I did, I would count the day as a success because I have made personal accomplishments. Everything else I do for the day flows out of the way I start my day. Leaders know that their day is a product of their disciplined routine.*

In her breakthrough research that turned into a TED Talk, and a best-selling book, Angela Duckworth,[165] breaks down what it takes to be extraordinary. She explains her comprehensive study of leaders from various fields showed that they all disciplined themselves through routine. Angela explains what makes people extraordinary is their GRIT, otherwise known as determination, that leads them to hours and hours of "*routined*" days. Without exception, extraordinary people are disciplined creatures of habit.

Her analysis of what it takes to become an exceptional leader debunks the idea of a Genius Gene or some Genetic Code that is required for greatness. Duckworth concludes that passion, and perseverance are some of the most valuable variables in a human. When coupled with discipline the combination is a formula for continued improvement.

In his book, "*The 7 Habits of Highly Effective People*," the late Stephen Covey suggests that leaders ask themselves questions to help them prioritize around what is most important.[166] I have used these questions myself to help me uncover where my priorities lie. I believe they are extremely valuable, so I have listed them here for you to use when determining how you might organize your day.

- Question 1: What one thing could you do that you aren't doing now that, if you did it on a regular basis, would make a tremendous positive difference in your personal life?

- Question 2: What one thing in your business or your professional life would bring similar results?

Your use of these questions to organize your priorities will give you essential items to build into your disciplined routine. If you find that you have problems with prioritization, I cannot recommend Stephen Covey's book highly enough. If you have it on your shelf, take it down and re-read it again.

These are questions that leaders should revisit often when they are unclear if they are making enough progress. Sometimes just revisiting our priorities can save us from questioning our chosen path. If we have discipline around a given set of worthy priorities, it is almost impossible to not make progress. This discipline helps us turn each day into a small win. When we begin to stack up small wins, week after week, it is inevitable that we will begin to show marked progress.

When others witness a disciplined leader, they see consistency. They can't help but notice a person who is passionate about making progress. Being consistent is one of the greatest traits a leader can exhibit. When a leader is consistent, the people around the leader feel safe and free to operate in their strengths.

Discipline breeds discipline.

A disciplined body and mind help a leader run at optimal levels, and when leaders run at optimal levels, everyone around them takes notice of the habits, and discipline spreads.

I suggested before to Google a few leaders you would like to test this theory on, so in my research, I did the same. While I was writing this book, Jeff Bezos became the wealthiest man in the world. He also does some great things with his profits. He wants to help the unfortunate. But he is also an inventor and optimizer, and a visionary to add to it all. Let's take a look at his published routine.[167]

1. He wakes early up and puts first-things-first by spending time alone in reading.

2. He spends quality time with those he is closest to.

3. His "Hi I.Q." meetings to start around 10:00 a.m.

4. The rest of his day is organized around priorities.

5. By 5:00 p.m., he winds things down to move on to his evening routine.

Bezos, in a CNBC interview, explains that he reserves his energy for what is most important – "Think about it, as a senior executive, what do you really get paid to do? As a senior executive, you get paid to make a small number of high quality decisions. Your job is not to make thousands of decisions every day."[168]

He went on to explain that even his sleep routine is disciplined. Bezos makes sure that he gets 8 hours of sleep per night and shares that when he is able to stay disciplined with this routine, everyone around him wins.

Benjamin Franklin led on many fronts in history and his hard work and disciplined learning have impacted the world greatly. Let's take a look at his published routine.[169]

1. He would wake by 5:00 a.m.

2. Franklin started his day with prayer. He was a known believer.

3. By 8:00 a.m., he would engulf himself in some type of reading.

4. There was a period of reflection for Franklin daily in which he ranked himself on his self-published virtues.

5. He made sure to eat a breakfast and then work till noon.

6. From noon to 2:00 p.m. was additional study then work commenced from 2:00 p.m. until 6:00 p.m.

Bezos and Franklin, though separated by two centuries, dealt with time in the same manner – by managing it through a personal disciplined routine. They were disciplined with their most valuable and scarce resource – Time! They stacked up small wins until they turned into big wins. They placed their most valuable tasks at the start of the day, and both of them invested in themselves by reading in the morning. Notice that both Bezos and Franklin reserved themselves for personal growth first. Their schedule paid themselves first through personal enrichment – Bezos with the people most important to him and Franklin with reflecting on his virtues. After their schedules allowed for personal wins, they moved to output or production – the doing of tasks.

Studying the routines of great leaders can help us develop a format for the way we build out our disciplined routines. We do not have to go at it alone, and the great truth about discipline is that it is available to everyone who will seek it diligently.

Sadly for most people, the ability to discipline themselves so that they can focus on what is most important, has become an elusive thing of the past. The never-ending chimes and vibrations of incoming phone calls, emails and tweets are robbing people of their ability to prioritize and accomplish what is most fundamental to success.

Leaders cannot fall into the trap of walking with the crowd of distracted people who are endlessly herding through life! A leader's discipline is a matter of significance, and if they will harness its power, it will reward them greatly.

29. Perseverance

"Perseverance is not a long race: It is many short races one after another."
Walter Elliot[170]

It takes stamina to continue pushing past our predefined limits. Therefor perseverance can make a big difference in the life of a leader.

For most today, perseverance is a thing of the past because of the incessant stimuli that distracts the average human who is burdened with 20,000 thoughts per hour. Our mind has the processing power to rival a supercomputer. But hour after hour, our mind can absorb stimuli and change directions over and over until we end up exhausted and frustrated with zero productivity to show for our time.

Once a leader has determined their vision and developed a plan to pursue it, they will need to strengthen their ability to persevere. Having a life plan or written life purpose statement will help leaders focus on what matters most and deflect the things that do not align with their purpose.

I have become more and more impressed with endurance athletes. I have many friends who participate in triathlons and distance running because of the mental toughness that it takes to accomplish endurance challenges like the Ironman® or similar challenges. These endurance challenges are not won on the day of the race, they are won in the perseverance through the training regimen prior to race day.

To accomplish anything great two ingredients are necessary, and they are focus and endurance.

Make no mistake, leadership is an endurance sport! Both focus and endurance are necessary for a leader to master once they have determined they will live a life of significance.

The military is a great training ground for perseverance, because it is required, and even demanded. Servicemen and women are constantly presented with obstacles. It is the constant conquering of obstacles that has enabled the U.S. Military to become one of the strongest and most capable militaries in the world.

For our military members, perseverance begins in boot camp or "*Basic Training.*" From day one of boot camp, the soldier is presented with obstacle after obstacle with which their mental and physical toughness is tested. Some persevere, and some crack under the pressure. Those who crack are sent home with a handful of regrets.

> *I personally remember the shock the minute I arrived at boot camp. As a "Recruit," the title we are given in basic, the first obstacle one must overcome is the fear of no longer having any control over what will happen next. When I stepped off of the bus in August of 1999 at Naval Recruit Training Command Great Lakes, I was greeted by a senior enlisted drill instructor screaming in my face.*

> *The prevailing message to the recruits is, "You are weak and you will never make it through this hell hole." From that moment forward I began to question whether I could endure what came next, and the tough part was not knowing.*

Leaders have to overcome the same thing, because they are naturally out front and are continually being confronted with things that are out of their control. Leaders must endure the pressure of internal and external factors that test their ability to accept uncontrollable situations.

Ultimately, the success of any organization or team rests on the shoulders of the leader. This pressure can be debilitating, and while most leaders are not being yelled at by a drill instructor, they are often under fire from a bad customer or toxic employee. Perseverance is crucial for leaders, because they must be able to overtake the obstacles they are confronted with.

> *I remember the rigor of boot camp, the grueling eight weeks, and the mental toughness I had to develop to keep from breaking down psychologically and spiritually. I remember marching along with fifty other recruits. We would march everywhere in boot camp. I recall many times that I was so physically and mentally exhausted, that while I was marching, I would fall asleep and stumble out of formation. I remember being so exhausted in boot camp that I and a few other brave souls would sneak off to the laundry room which was in the far corner of our barracks. We would lay our tired bodies on bags of dirty laundry. This was a high risk nap, and a few recruits were caught sleeping and were punished by being ASMO'd. The military is notorious for using acronyms to aid in remembering crucial terms. This one stood for Assignment Memorandum Order.*

> *When a recruit in the Navy screwed up, they were threatened with being set back two weeks in boot camp, and this is what the famous acronym ASMO stood for in the minds of recruits. NAVY drill instructors struck fear into the hearts of all recruits by threatening to ASMO them back two weeks. They even brainwashed us by saying if you do this or that, you will be ASMO'd. For example, there was a staircase leading up to the top floor of the barracks*

where I was assigned. The railing that led to the staircase was polished brass. These bars were known as "the ASMO bars" because if we touched them and were caught, we would be ASMO'd back two weeks. This was nothing more than another mental obstacle all recruits had to overcome to succeed in basic training.

It took a certain level of perseverance to graduate boot camp in the NAVY just as it takes a certain level of perseverance to accomplish any daunting task.

Leaders must be ready for challenges. They can do this by continuing to build their perseverance, so when they are confronted with obstacles, they can muster the necessary mental, physical and spiritual toughness it takes to overcome the challenges they are facing. Just like creative writing, calculus, or any other learned skill, endurance can be learned, and built upon. Leaders who are smart and want to prepare themselves for the next level will invest in building their endurance, so that when they are confronted with an obstacle they can be victorious instead of being stopped in their tracks.

Leaders should train their physical, mental and spiritual endurance by setting "*stretch goals*" in their life.

A "*stretch goal*" is something that has never been attained by that individual leader.

By setting "stretch goals," we can build our base of perseverance. Here are some examples.

- A mental stretch goal can be reading a number of books per month.

- A physical goal can be running a marathon in a set amount of time in a given year.

- Spiritual endurance is just as important as the physical and mental components of endurance. A spiritual stretch goal could be to pray or meditate daily for a set number of minutes.

Stretching ourselves to go further than we have gone in the past will help us attain new levels of competence. If we continue to stretch ourselves over and over, we will be ready when we are confronted with a new challenge instead of being crushed by the fear that comes with it.

Persevering through trying times will help leaders see challenges with a new paradigm. Once a leader has accepted and conquered a few obstacles in their life, they can see future obstacles as just another test of endurance.

Persevering allows us to rid ourselves of spiritual, mental and physical blocks.

Perseverance is essential for a leader to continue to evolve, so the next time you are confronted with an obstacle, remember that the obstacle is the way. It is only a temporary road block, and on the other side of it, you will find confidence, strength and resilience.

30. Leaders and Villains

"The only thing we have to fear is fear itself"
Franklin D. Roosevelt[171]

Franz Kafka was a novelist and short story writer who was widely regarded as one of the major figures of 20th Century literature. He wrote a short parable named *"Before the Law,"* published first in 1915. Let me summarize the story for you.

> *A young man came to a doorway in his journey that he desired and prayed for admittance through. But standing in his way was a fierce and intimidating doorkeeper who was blocking his travel. The man knew that his destiny awaited him somewhere beyond the door, so he humbly asked the doorkeeper to allow him to pass through the doorway.*
>
> *The doorkeeper replied, ""I cannot allow you to enter at this time."*
> *The young man thought about the response and*

asked, "Will there be a time in the future that I can enter?"

The doorkeeper responded with a cold, "Maybe."

Just then, the young man noticed that the actual door was open, so he moved closer to the entrance. The doorkeeper moved slightly to the side so that the young man could at least peer through the entryway. As the young man moved closer to the door, the keeper in an authoritative, antagonistic voice said,

"If you are so drawn to it, just try to go in despite my veto. But take note: I am powerful. And I am only the least of the doorkeepers. From hall to hall there is one doorkeeper after another, each one more powerful than the last."

The young man crumbled in trepidation and fear, and he decided it would be too great a challenge to enter the door. And instead of focusing on his destiny that awaited through the door, he began to fix his eyes on the doorkeeper. He noticed that the guard was now scarier than ever – his face and nose were long and sharp, his beard pointed, his long black fur coat covered what must be a menacing body of destruction – and the young man became paralyzed with fear.

The doorkeeper, satisfied with the young man's cowering fear, grinned, and reached for his stool. He *put it beside the door and told the youngster, "You can wait here beside the doorway."*

The young man waited for hours. The hours turned into days, the days into months, and the months quickly become years. Year after year, the man asked, "Can I enter yet?"

The doorkeeper's only response was, "Not yet."

The years went by, and the young man grew old and became exceedingly desperate. He tried everything from begging, to bribing the doorkeeper to let him through the door; the very door that he knew led to his destiny.

The man who once was young, was now old and near death. He began to question the doorkeeper, "Surely it is unfair that I have waited all these years to reach my destiny, and your only response is 'not yet!'"

The old man was now confined to lying down by the door because the years of waiting have worn down his body.

Finally, he asked the doorkeeper, "Surely you are not this way with everyone who comes to the door; why have you tortured me all these years?"
The doorkeeper seeing now that the man was close to death stooped down and decided, once and for all, to tell him the truth of matter. The menacing

doorkeeper bent down and roared in the dying man's ear, **"This door was never made for others to enter it. It was made only for you to walk through it and find your destiny, but fear held you back, and now I am going to shut the door!"**

At some point in our life, all of us find ourselves sitting by the door afraid of what might happen if we face our villains. Our fears are often exponentially greater than our true dangers. <u>As leaders we need to challenge our fears in whatever form they show up</u>.

I call this *"Confronting our Villains."*

Every human has at least one "villain" that will show up and remind them of all the negative scary things that could happen if they chase their dream. This causes fear to well up and limit them.

These villains usually lurk in the shadows and only show themselves just long enough for us to question whether they are real or not. They peak their masked faces out when we get close to a breakthrough. They remind us of the various reasons we cannot succeed as a leader, hit a milestone or break through to the next level of operating.

These villains keep us in a defensive posture, and every time they rear their ugly imaginary faces, we are tempted to retreat.

But, we get to choose if they can be stopped and confronted. We decide if they are unmasked and get revealed for what they are....just imaginary fears. Most of the time, we create these villains and allow them to manifest in our lives.

> *I live in The Woodlands, Texas, a heavily wooded area: hence the name. There are all sorts of creatures that wander out on to the paths I run on. In the past, I have killed copperhead snakes that I almost stepped on as I ran.*

> *One day while running, I heard and saw the bushes near me rustling a few times. I was spooked and jumped – only to look over and see a squirrel jumping too, because I spooked it. Here we were, man and squirrel jumping in fear!*

> *I thought to myself, "I have been through a war where people were shooting at me, but these squirrels are kicking my butt!"*

I came to the realization that for most of my life, I had been living in a scared, defensive posture. I began to envision a new posture where, instead, I would be ready to attack fears whenever they presented themselves. Until it happens to you, I guess you never know what a squirrel can bring out of you.

Leaders should develop the idea of attacking fears.

Most of the time when we explore our fears, we will realize that they are either imaginary, or they are manifestations of some past issue we have not yet addressed. I love the acronym for **FEAR**, (**F**alse **E**vidence **A**ppearing **R**eal).

Most of our fears are just squirrels in the bush!

I have learned that most of my fears, if metaphorically placed on a shelf for three to four days, will evaporate on their own. So when something creeps into my mind and worries me, I have developed a habit of telling myself, ***"Terry give this a few days, and it will be gone."***

The next time you catch yourself worrying about something try this....Tell yourself, *"This fear is false; it will be gone in a few days."* To do it, you will need to make a choice not to think about the fear. It will keep coming back at you, and you will need to say to yourself, *'That's garbage and I don't need to dwell on it.'* Then choose to focus your mind on something else.

Keep the word *"garbage"* in your mind, and when the fear hits you again, toss it out the same way. Don't be surprised if you have to do this several dozen times. However, if you continue to set you fears aside, most of them will dissipate with this practice. Until a fear becomes a danger, we need to get rid of it.

> *I remember a time I became afraid for my life. It was the first time we had incoming missiles headed for our compound while engaged in the Iraq War. Once our intelligence unit discovered there were incoming missiles, they sounded a loud alarm. Then our U.S. forces fired off defensive missiles, called "Patriots,"*

that would meet the opponent's missile strike mid-air before they reached our troops. The first time this happened for me was in the dead of the night while I was fast asleep.

I remember being shaken awake by the percussion of the Patriot Missiles launching – it was loud and powerful, and it shook the ground. Then a loud siren went off signaling all the sleeping troops to run for the bomb shelters. I remember the first thought I had while experiencing this, "We are done for – we are all gonna die and lose the war." I immediately went into "Doomsday mode", where I thought...everyone is toast, life is over, and the enemy wins. These thoughts were completely founded on fears.

This type of reaction is typically how we handle fears, but we do not have to let them rule us. People are looking to us for an example. When fear strikes, all eyes point to the leader. Leaders must be able to combat fear with their courage, rationale, and faith. They must be able to take fearful thoughts captive and shelf them.... Then they must come up with their own plan of attack, otherwise known as a "*counterstrike*," once they have assessed that the fear is legitimate, and not just a squirrel in the bush.

A leader must know how to combat fears when they are real.

The simplest and best way to garner strength is by reaching out and asking for it. Most of the ancient Eastern

Philosophies tell us that asking for help is a show of weakness and a burden to others, but this is false. The best leaders have wise counsel to which they can turn to when they are in need of strength. When a leader asks for help, it gives others an opportunity to serve and partner in the success of those they care about most.

> *A business partner of mine was recently struggling. I could discern that something was haunting her, so I asked her how she was doing personally. At first, she said that everything was alright. But I knew something was bothering her because her face and actions were telling a different story.*

Inward fears, and turmoil always present themselves outwardly. The ancient Hebrew Proverb says, "*Above all else, guard your heart, for everything you do flows from it,*"[172] and whether the heart is broken or blissful, our actions will share the condition of what is going on internally.

> *As I pressed a little deeper with my friend, she began to open up. She shared that she was being pressured by her parents, and her husband, to have kids, but she did not feel it was the right time. This led to tension in her life, so she and her husband decided to divorce after nine years.*
>
> *She went on to explain that while growing up in China, her parents taught her that telling others about her problems was a sign of weakness and it was a burden on others. This was a little heartbreaking for me to hear. I told her she should*

share what she was going through with her closest
friends whom she trusts, because they can be a
source of strength for her. Shortly after our
conversation, I began receiving messages from my
friend reaching out for help...she is stronger because
of it.

As leaders, we have an obligation to help bear the burdens
of others and walk with them through their challenges. We
should also realize that most of us will end up in a place
where we don't have a clear solution in front of us. So
sometimes we have to ask for help! Often, all we need is the
collective strength of someone in our corner to spur us on to
defeating the greatest villains in our life.

Take a moment to write down the names of two or three
people you will reach out to for strength the next time you
are faced with a situation that you cannot handle alone.

_____

_____

_____

_____

Now promise yourself that you will rely on others for help for
these two reasons.

- We need wise counsel in our life to help us through
  challenges.

- Asking for help is not a show of weakness, but in fact, it is a way to garner strength from others.

Lastly, there is a benefit for those we ask for help. When we open up and ask for strength from others, it gives them the opportunity to serve us and create deeper relationship with us.

31. Leaders and Limits

"Life begins at the end of your comfort zone."
Neale Donald Walsch[173]

Leaders continually push their limits and challenge their own potential.

We, as a people, understand that most will never come close to reaching their full potential. We ask ourselves the question, "What is the difference between us and Einstein, or the endurance athlete, or the CEO running a Fortune 100® company?"

The quicker that we realize our self-imposed limits are what's holding us back, the faster we can begin to narrow the gap between our current state, and our true potential.

About 15 years ago I saw a quote that caught my eye, it said, *"Life isn't about finding yourself, it is about creating yourself."*

The quote was on a mug in a coffee shop, so I bought it, and I still have it to this day.

- It reminds me to set my limits, and to continually challenge them.

- It also reminds me that no one else has a say in my potential.

- Finally, it reminds me the difference between a wanderer who spends a lifetime trying to figure out who they are, and the leader who decides who they will become and then chases that vision, constantly setting and surpassing new limits.

Leaders must realize we are what we decide to become and that if we push our limits, we can achieve greatness.

"Limits, like fears, are often an illusion"
Michael Jordan[174]

Leaders understand that pursuing their true potential is something they can transfer to others. They can show others how to live a life that continually pursues greatness. Leaders should want to travel and progress with others to help them max out their limits. One of the greatest gifts a leader can receive is "Thanks" from another for helping them achieve a new limit.

Success in isolation is a lack of leadership. If a leader hits thirty percent of their goals and helps ten others do the same, they are more successful than if they hit 100 percent of their own goals in isolation. If you have trouble believing this, do the math, and remember that leaders in isolation are not true leaders.

> *The other day I got "a wild hair" after listening to an endurance athlete who pushed himself to run 205 miles without stopping. I took off on a run and decided I was going to push myself too.*
>
> *Until that day, the most I had ever run was a half marathon, 13.1 miles, back in 2007. It took me 7 months to train for that half marathon. I used a training schedule that gradually prepared me for the final distance.*
>
> *This time, more ten years later, I wondered if I could push myself to run 13.1 miles without all the training I'd done years before, so I decided I would give it a shot. At about mile eight, my body was screaming at me to quit, and the outsides of my knees were aching, but I pushed on. At mile ten, I told myself that I had made it, and I knew that nothing was going to stop me from completing my "Half Marathon Whim." I finished the run in just over two hours beating my marathon time for which I had previously trained for so long.*
>
> *I had not run more than six miles in over ten years before that week. For some reason I was able to will myself through that run without any training.*

I don't recommend doing this type of silly challenge, because for the next three days, I could barely walk.... The sides of my knees felt like someone had pounded them with a hammer for hours straight!

But this challenge was beneficial for me because it stretched me and took me to a new level of thinking.

I began to question whether I was pushing myself hard enough over the last few years. I realized that in business, and my personal life I had some untapped potential. That day something clicked for me mentally, and I decided I would begin pushing myself harder in all areas of my life.

The next Sunday, our pastor asked us to write our greatest fear on a card that was provided for us. I thought for a minute and realized my greatest fear was a very significant one.

On the card I wrote, "I fear that I will not live up to my calling and potential."

I knew from that moment on I needed to continue to stretch and push myself as a leader and encourage others to do the same.

Leaders know they must continue to challenge themselves, and also challenge the people around them to redefine limits and push themselves further than they've ever imagined possible. Leaders have an innate desire to achieve their goals, and they know they have to push themselves continually by facing, and overcoming greater challenges. We have to take ourselves to new limits, and break through them, before we can achieve new opportunities and growth. Some people decide to grow alone, but leaders know they have to challenge others to grow together – this is the essence of true leadership.

There is strength in numbers, and when people band together, there is great synergy created that adds fuel for growth. The evolving leader knows when the right people come together and concert their efforts, there is nothing that cannot be accomplished.

> "Never doubt that a small group of thoughtful, committed citizens can change the world: indeed, it is the only thing that ever has."
>
> Margaret Mead[175]

Recently, I heard Tyler Perry[176] speak about leadership and what it means to be a leader. He passionately reminded the audience, "We are not our own when we are leaders. This journey is not only ours – there are many people we can hold the door for."

Tyler told a story about when he was just starting out as an actor.

> He was doing theater acting at the time, and he would envision sellout crowds. He went on to share that sometimes no one would show up for his performance, but he decided that would not limit his dreams. He explained that his dreams were the only

thing that kept him going since he could not rely on reality: a "No Audience" performance was way too depressing. Tyler pushed forward until people began to show up. Before he knew it, his dreams were his reality, and he was now performing for packed audiences.

Tyler continued to dream big and envision what could be – instead of letting reality limit his thinking. Tyler Perry now employs thousands of people in a studio he has built from his dreams and hard work. When Tyler talks to groups of leaders, he shares that he now realizes the people who work with him have destinies tied to him, and leaders need to realize they are a part of something bigger than themselves. Tyler's talk ended with him saying that we as leaders need to "*Carry love in our hearts as we lead.*"

Leaders must allow their dreams to carry them past reality. It takes an unreal level of thinking to make real breakthroughs. Albert Einstein knew this to be truth when he said, "*You cannot solve a problem using the same level or basis of thought used to create it.*"[177]

This statement can be applied to any *status quo* by realizing we can never push past our limits with our limited thinking. Leaders must think past their current limits, and inspire others to do the same, so that together they can achieve new level of success.

32. Leaders and Collaboration

"We don't know what we don't know."
Bob Koenig[178]

There is brilliance in simplicity, and sometimes it is true that ignorance is bliss. But leaders need to understand that the fastest way out of ignorance is through collaboration.

When I first heard the quote, *"We don't know what we don't know,"* I felt I had just recognized a massive void in my life that I had been unaware of my entire life. The idea is brilliantly simplistic, and if we will accept the fact that we know so little, it will make it easy for us to understand our need for collaboration. All leaders have *"Knowledge Gaps,"* areas that we don't quite understand. And if we recognize and accept this, we can begin to give others the opportunity to fill in these gaps. We can never understand leadership unless we accept the fact that collaboration is key to helping everyone advance.

In their book *"Leaders, Myth and Reality,"*[179] the authors share, *"Leadership is coproduced by leaders and followers, emerging between the influential and charismatic who crave it and the hopeful and fearful who demand it."*

This definition shows both the need from the masses for leadership, and the supply of charisma, and skill, from those who step up to lead. This explains that an interdependent relationship must exist for leadership to even happen. It amplifies the meaning of collaboration which is a *"co-laboring"* between two distinct parties. If we look at the inputs of leadership as a collaboration, it will keep us rooted in the right paradigm. It will keep the leader and their team somewhat dependent on each other.

The collaboration mindset will guard leaders from making decisions without the right inputs.

Decisions made in a vacuum happen in one of two ways.

- The first way is they are made alone by a leader without consultation.

- The second way is they are made in *"groupthink"* due to leaders surrounding themselves with people who are not diverse in thinking, experienced with collaboration, or who are afraid to share a new idea.

The very best leaders start a meeting of the minds with questions. Leaders are problem solvers. They solve diverse problems such as: sales, human resources, brand clarity, culture, and much more. Instead of asking how we solve a problem, some of the best leaders begin to add to their understanding by asking the brightest around them, *"What don't we know about the problem?"*

When we ask *"What don't we know?"* instead of *"How do we fix it?"* we begin to fill in *"Knowledge Gaps"* around a problem.

The idea that the leader should make decisions fast and fearless is a poor one at best. There is a saying in military, especially during war, *"Battles are won in the general's tent."* This idea is a little misleading because it paints the picture of a single general hunched over a dimly lit table, late at night devising battle plans with a few terrain maps and a copy of *The Art of War.* This idea is far from the truth and what really happens in war time.

The generals have intelligence teams who gather information, package it, and then present it in a concise manner. They receive threat assessments before making decisions to attack. They ask over and over, "What do we not know about the problem?" before they create the battle plan. The truth is that the door to the general's tent has a constant flow of diverse information being exchanged from sources outside of the general's own knowledge base. To get a diverse knowledge base, we must have people of diverse thinking, and **we as leaders must be okay with being challenged.**

Leaders should see their knowledge gaps as a temporary weakness that can only be solved by pulling together a diverse team who will challenge their thinking and bring fresh ideas and details to the "information pool."

An "*information pool*" is a collective set of knowledge and experience that helps a team prepare solutions to problems.

The solutions then create the way forward.

Our job as an evolving leader is to create an environment where ideas freely flow from our team. When we receive an idea that seems unconventional, our first response should normally be, "*Tell me more about the idea.*"

When we present our team with open ended questions, it gives the team an opportunity to collaborate. It also allows for expansion in our perspectives. Without new perspective and fresh ideas, a team and what they offer becomes stagnant as the world continues to change around them.

> "Great minds discuss ideas; average minds discuss events; small minds discuss people."
> Eleanor Roosevelt[180]

Can you imagine what would happen without teams and people discussing new ideas? We would be stuck in the dark ages as a human race. There would be no vehicles, no communication devices, we'd still be camping under the stars and eating only what we can catch.

Until our ideas are challenged – either by another person or something greater than ourselves, we are stuck in the past forever. Until the late President Kennedy challenged NASA and the American people with completing a mission to the moon, we were mere Earthlings.

Can you imagine what people thought the day President Kennedy stated that we were going to the moon?

Think about this idea from the perspective of the person who heard it for the first time:

> 'Wait a minute, we are going to put people into a massive metal tube, then we will fill it with enough explosives to blast the crew and cargo out of Earth's atmosphere. Then they will travel in zero gravity to the moon, the very object that lights our night and creates a gravitational pull on our oceans. The trip will take an unknown number of days, and the people in the massive rocket will not be able to breathe air while they are gone unless it is manufactured for them. Then....the same crew will fly back to Earth for a crash landing in the ocean."

Does that sound possible or crazy?

Sounds a little nutty, even to me – today. This idea would never have become history if President Kennedy had not surrounded himself with a team who thought differently than himself. But he did just that, then he listened to their futuristic thinking. The famous moonshot that catapulted the American people ahead of the known world would still be an idea today without a team of collaborators who challenged the thinking of the free world's leader.

"Many ideas grow better when transplanted into
another mind than the one where they sprang up."
Oliver Wendell Holmes[181]

The people surrounding you are dying to have their ideas heard. They want to add value and feel like they are more than just programed *"worker bees."* When people's ideas are heard, the uniqueness of their identity and their contribution is validated.

Think about it – the human mind is an idea factory. When we take the limits off of that factory, it produces the type of thinking that leads to breakthroughs. A culture of fresh thinking and new ideas creates a breeding ground for innovation. Think about some of these fresh ideas that have challenged conventional thinking: autonomous cars, nuclear power, artificial intelligence, embryonic stem cells and digital currency.

These ideas are modern day phenomena because of leaders and teams thinking about what **could be**. They came from an environment of collaboration and diverse ideas. They will soon be challenged again. They will become ideas of the past so long as leaders continue to evolve their thinking, create innovative environments, and embrace a culture of collaboration.

When leaders close the door to collaboration, they create decision-making silos, and simultaneously create a culture lacking trust. They cut themselves off from the next great idea and toss synergistic thought out the window.

What has challenged your thinking lately? If the answer is "*Nothing*," there is a problem with your team. It may be unhealthy.

One way we can invite new ideas into our team is by holding brainstorming sessions. This can be formal or informal. It simply consists of the leader inviting collaboration into the current operation. It can be as simple as getting a team of people together with the sole focus of creating new ideas around solving a problem. All we need are willing participants, a culture of collaboration, and fresh ideas. It is relatively free, and it may lead to the next "*moonshot*" idea for you and for the people you surround yourself with.

> "*Talent wins games, but teamwork and intelligence win championships.*"
> Michael Jordan[182]

Michael Jordan is a classic example of a solo superstar who evolved over time into a world class collaborator. At some point in Jordan's career, he learned what collaboration meant for a team.

Collaboration defies conventional thinking and logical math.

It says that "*one plus one plus one equals much more than three,*" when teamwork is embraced. It says that the energy and ingenuity of people working together is much greater than the sum of their individual contributions.

When we study Michael Jordan, we see possibly the most talented basketball player to ever step foot on the basketball court. He seemed to gracefully float through the air to dunk the basketball. But at some point in his career, Jordan realized that by keeping the ball to himself, he robbed his team of synergy and championship opportunities.

On September 11th of 2009 Jordan was inducted into the NBA Hall of Fame.[183] He gave a speech during the ceremony that began with referencing the people he collaborated with.

> "I told all my friends I was just gonna come up here and say 'thank you' and walk off. I can't. There's no way. I got too many people I gotta thank. In all the videos, you never just saw me; you saw Scottie Pippen."

His speech was roughly twenty-three minutes, and during his speech he could have talked about all he had accomplished over his illustrious career. But instead he mentioned by name forty players, coaches, mentors, friends, and family members that he collaborated with over the length of his career. Jordan's talk was about the people who shared the journey with him. Jordan openly rebuked a person in the audience who once tried to say it was the organization that wins championships. Michael corrected him to never take the championship win from the team.

Jordan spent a lot of time addressing Pat Riley, who was an opposing coach who gave Jordan some of the fiercest trials of his career. Jordan spent time thanking him for the competition that allowed him to rise as a champion. He thanked Pat for sending great competitors and strategies against him. He mentioned the time when Pat would not let Charles Oakley, one of Pat's players, and Jordan's best friend, eat lunch with him. Jordan said…. "*That made me better.*"

It was even with his opponents that Jordan seemed to work with to make himself better. In thanking his competition, he said, "*I just so happen to be a friendly guy. I get along with everybody, but at the same time when the light comes on I'm just as competitive as anybody you know. So you guys I have to say thank you very much for that motivation that I desperately needed.*"

Over the course of Jordan's career, his evolution as a leader helped him realize that collaboration is the key to success. It took Jordan and his team seven years to win their first championship.[184] When we look at the seasons Jordan and his team won championships, we see a trend in his individual points scored per season. During the years 1988, 89, and 90, Jordan scored an average of 2,751 points over the entire seasons. During the years 91, 92, and 93 Jordan's points dropped to an average of 2,508 per season a decline of 243 points over the previous three seasons, but that is when Jordan and his team of collaborators won three NBA

Championships in a row. Together, Jordan and his team also won championship titles in 1996, 97, and 98. Again Jordan's individual scoring was a lower average per season at 2,426, but his team participated more, and they took six championships.

We, as evolving leaders do not have to be world-class athletes, presidents, or military commanders to begin to collaborate. But if we have a desire to share similar successes to that which: Michael Jordan, President Kennedy, and General McChrystal have accomplished, we must take notes from their greatest leadership lessons.

All of these high performing leaders knew that to get where they wanted to go, they also needed a team to help get them there. Each of these leaders discovered that collaboration was a tipping point in their personal success and the success of their team. If we, as evolving leaders, will begin to place great emphasis on collaboration, we will make strides toward our success, and we will help many others along the way.

33. Leaders and Choices

"All of us were given an incredible power that will define us, and the power is our ability to choose."

Terry Weaver

There is a well-known story of two men, Carl Mead and Tom White, who together taught the world the difference between "purpose" and "achievement." Their story is believed to have saved many years of directionless wandering for millions of people.

> *Carl and Tom grew up as childhood friends and were almost inseparable. They played, did sports, and took up new hobbies together. But most importantly they dreamt together. They shared dreams of growing up and becoming successful one day. As they started to mature, their ideas of success began to diverge. Carl had ideas of going to college*

and moving into corporate America in hopes of climbing the ladder to success. But Tom dreamt of building a business that would one day employ others. Tom's business model was simple. He would help put good into the world by serving others through business.

As the boys grew into men, Carl became very pragmatic in his thinking; he all but demanded his friend Tom do the same, and follow in his footsteps. Carl explained, "Tom you have to follow a proven method to reach success – chasing your dreams is Hollywood stuff."

But Tom rejected the idea of a herd mentality and told Carl, "If the masses are doing things the same way, there must be opportunity in what people are not doing."

Unfortunately, as their ideals became more and more different, their relationship became strained.

As for Tom, he believed he had a unique purpose and that he was given the ability to dream for a reason, so at age eighteen he started his very first business. He began as a handy-man in the construction industry repairing fences and doing small projects in residential and commercial markets. Two years into Tom's venture, he became busy enough to start subcontracting work out to small construction companies. And after just five years in business, Tom had a company that employed a half-dozen people.

Carl, on the other hand, went away to college and then on to law school. Upon graduating in the top ten-percent of his class, he had multiple job offers awaiting his consideration. Carl believed he had made it to the good life. He accepted a six figure salary upon graduation and found himself quickly immersed in case work for the firm's partners while studying for the bar exam in the evenings. After five years as an associate, Carl was recommended for partnership at the firm. This promised him a cut from all profits the firm made, so he jumped at the offer. After making partner, Carl began to immerse himself even deeper into his work.

Elsewhere, Tom continued to slowly grow his company, and by the time his company was just ten years old, he decided to focus on giving back to his community and to those who were less fortunate than he was. By this time, Tom had a thriving enterprise, so he began incentivizing his people to get involved in local charities and give back. This was not only fulfilling for his employees, but it also helped fulfill his dreams of living a purposeful life, and it fueled his passion to continue growing his company.

By no means was Tom's journey easy. Tom was known to put in upwards of seventy hours per week running his company; he also took time in the evenings to coach his son's soccer team, and he volunteered at his church at least once per week. But even though Tom was working upwards of 15 hours per day, he was purpose-filled and loved what he was doing, so it wasn't overwhelming. Tom's life confirmed the old saying, "If you find a way to make money doing something you love, you will never work another day in your life."

Meanwhile, Carl began to feel the pressure of being a partner at a prestigious law firm. He became very stressed with his firm's cases, so he began working weekends to show he was committed. He was determined to increase the partner's year-end payouts at all personal costs. Carl began working on his cases at home which robbed time from his wife and newborn baby. He justified his decision of putting in the extra hours by saying, "I will work hard now, so I can retire young and spend as much time with my family as they need."

Pressure only mounted for Carl; he took up drinking four to five scotches in the evening just to unwind a bit from the stress of the day and get a little reprieve. Carl's bad habits turned into weeks of hazy stressed out work frenzies, and his lifestyle took a toll on his young family.

Carl's desire for success only fueled his workaholic lifestyle. The divide widened between Carl and his wife and now five year old daughter. The tension and fighting between he and his wife grew to the point where he'd had enough. Carl decided he needed a break from his family. He told himself, "If I don't get a break, I will lose everything that I worked so hard to build."

Carl rented a city apartment closer to the firm's office, so he could focus on work. He convinced himself that the break from his family would only last until his caseload became manageable.

Back in Tom's world, his business took a turn for the worst. During the winter of 2009, his construction business was hit hard by the nationwide recession. There was financial pressure on the business, and his employees began to question if their jobs were safe. The company's backlog of work dwindled, and Tom struggled to make payroll. Tom felt he was being tested and began to question whether he made the right decision to chase his dreams. He often remembered Carl's words, "Tom, you need to take the proven route to success....go to school, work hard and climb the corporate ladder."

Despite the financial woes, Tom held on tight and relied on his faith and his dreams of living a purposeful life. Tom's financial situation finally hit a point where he would have to begin laying off employees. Some of his people were in their thirteenth year with the company, and they were more like family than co-workers. In 2010, Tom made a selfless and risky decision to put a second mortgage on his home which enabled him to keep his long-time employees on the payroll. Tom told himself and his team, "I will do everything I can to keep this company and my people working."

The respect and dedication of his employees grew tremendously. Fortunately for Tom and his employees, they weathered the storm, and the construction market recovered. Tom and his people believed there was a guardian up above looking out for them.

Back at the firm, Carl's stress continued to mount. At one point, He and his partners worked twenty-three days straight, which included a stint straight through Christmas. Then, in the spring of 2010, Carl was served with divorce paperwork from his wife. This only fueled Carl's habits of overworking by day and drinking in the evenings to relax. He handled his divorce like most other cases – with limited emotion and a fire burning in his belly to win. He fought back the personal pain with work, and more scotch.

At this point in the story, I will pause briefly for a "*Spoiler Alert.*" These characters do not actually exist, but the situations actually do. We all know people who fit into this story. The story is a fable about the trap that too many ambitious people find themselves falling prey. Today's idea of "*Climbing the ladder of success,*" is one of the biggest lies ever told to mankind.

As the fable goes, Tom decided there was a unique purpose he was designed to live out. He decided he would chase his passion and seek fulfillment. Carl, on the other hand, bought into climbing the ladder to success and putting his career and personal desires before everything else. Tom invested his time and talent in relationships and caring for others, while Carl isolated and pushed his relationships to the side so he could chase the illusive idea of success.

If this story resonates with you, and like me, you see yourself resembling some piece of these characters, I challenge you to begin to think about your life as a masterpiece. Think of your life as a painting that is being brushed onto a canvas every day.

Now fast forward to the end of your life, and try to envision the picture that might be painted if you stay on the path you are currently taking.

Will the picture be one you are proud to hang on the halls of history?

Will the painting be revered as a work of art?

Will others smile when they see the picture of your life, or will it bring sadness to you and its viewers?

The truth is, we are all painting a picture that will be hung on the walls of history. Towards the end of our lives, we will spend much time looking at the picture we have painted with our life. We will ask ourselves questions like, *"Why did I make that brush stroke there, why didn't I paint a little more over here, and am I proud of my painting or deeply grieved by the way that it looks?"*

Let me clarify that it does not matter whether you take the corporate route or some other type of route towards what you view as success.

What matters most is your definition of success, how you get to it, and how many people you effect on your journey towards it.

Thankfully, we get to choose the life we will lead. This story parallels two lives, one who chooses to place success before everything else, and one who sacrifices and eventually builds something good by chasing his purpose. And while the characters are fictional, the principles which they are based on – are very real.

We all must choose which path we will pursue, either a life pointed at personal gain and success or a life pointed at helping others and fulfilling our purpose. Choose wisely!

It's time to take a reflective look at your life, and ask yourself these questions, then write the answers below:

Am I chasing success or moving towards purpose?

_____

_____

_____

Am I placing relationships as a necessity or as a priority?

_____

_____

_____

_____

Does my focus need to shift from my own personal gain to something more meaningful?

_____

_____

_____

_____

The Facts:

#1 It's never too late to make a change for the good. Countless leaders in the past have changed the course of history for millions in the latter years of their lives.

#2 There is no such thing as too small when you make a meaningful difference in your life or the lives of others. You can start making a meaningful change in the lives of

others by encouraging one person every week.
This could be as simple as writing a note to
someone who is struggling in life. You would
be amazed at the impact your words can make
on someone who needs them.

#3 *At the end of life, relationships matter most*.
Are relationships what matter most to you
today? What is the most common scene at the
hospital bedside towards the end of one's life?
It is loved ones gathered around sharing
memories with each other. It is bittersweet
hugs and kisses from family and friends who
are about to lose someone who was invested
in their life, or sadly, it is the lack of this
happening.

These questions and facts should challenge us to take
inventory of our lives. They will help us begin to evaluate
and possibly refocus our life's trajectory.

As we shift our priorities, we will learn that the quality of life
is determined by the quality of our relationships, and that as
our relationships with others grow, we too grow. Hopefully,
at some point, we will all realize we were placed on this
Earth for others. We are made for rich relationships with
friends, co-workers, our lovers and most importantly, our
Creator.

34. The Start

"The leader who refuses to move until the fear is gone will never move. Consequently, he will never lead….leadership is about moving boldly into the future in spite of uncertainty and risk. Without courage we simply accumulate a collection of good ideas and regrets."
Andy Stanley[185]

You may be wondering where to start your evolution as a leader.

I have great news for you! **You already have**.

You started a long time ago…. All of your experiences have brought you to today. Everything in your life has prepared you for this moment and now you get to decide how to live out today.

It all comes down to this moment…. It's the only one we have, and what we decide to do with it matters. Our moments build into minutes, minutes into hours, hours to days, and so forth. When we create a great set of days, weeks, then months, we soon can look back and see progress, but it all begins with this moment and what we decide to do with it.

> *I made a choice roughly six years ago to continue to evolve as a leader. I felt for a long time that I was living in a cage because I had an inner longing to do something greater than just punch a clock and go through the motions of life. Something greater was tapping me on the shoulder for a long time trying to wake me out of the mediocre slumber I was resting in. It took a while to build the confidence to act on my calling to live for something greater than myself, and I believe it would be a failure on my part not to share a little about my evolution as a leader.*

I believe the worst thing I could do for you is to present this book as some kind of easy *"How to do leadership"* manual.

> *The truth is I have made countless mistakes in my personal journey. I have failed relationships, addictions, periods of depression and much...much more.*

> *I came to a point in my life when I was about twenty-eight that I realized I was living a life of just barely surviving, and I made a choice to do something about it. I slowly started to evolve as a leader through whatever means I could find.*

*This, in itself, was a journey, and even though I
made a decision to improve, I was still faced with
much turmoil along the way. My life and all I went
through is for a different book. But the way I dug
myself out of the pit of despair is applicable to this
book and everyone reading it.*

So I will share the relevant ideas that got me to where I am
today. I know I must continue to evolve as a leader just as
all leaders should continue to evolve.

*This is how I began my evolution as a leader. I
started to cling to a power greater than myself. That
power for me is my Creator – God.*

Everything I have written in this book was inspired from my
journey, and it is my intention for it to be used to bring glory
to God. The greatest thing I have ever done is made a
choice to seek God intentionally and rely on Him for strength
and wisdom. The principles in this book are God's principles.
I reference men and women of the past, along with my own
experience to help bring them to life, but everything –
without exception written before this sentence was in some
form or fashion influenced by my faith in Christ.

Let me make it clear that whether you believe in a deity or
not, this book can help you evolve as a leader. This is why:
truth is truth, always – no matter the source. Principles are
enduring and they withstand the test of time. The principles I
have outlined in this book are nothing new under the sun. So

whether you are an atheist, agnostic, or some flavor of a religious type, these principles still apply to you and your life.

As for me, it is important to share the source of this book and the principles that are outlined in it, because I believe it would be incomplete without me doing so. In fact, the entire writing of this book was accomplished through a very rigorous, disciplined approach.

To this point in my writing, I have awakened every day at 4:00 a.m. to begin my daily routine. It always happens the exact same way. I start by reading scripture for roughly thirty minutes, and then I pray to God for thirty minutes. After my reading and prayer, I write for roughly ninety minutes. Every single day that I have written, I have asked God to help me construct the message you are now reading.

In addition to God's help, I have referenced over forty leadership books that I believe are some of the best ever written to pull from the generational wisdom we all have access to. I have studied leaders throughout time from the ancient Greek Socrates, to Michael Jordan. I have found many of the greatest leaders share similarities that can be organized into leadership principles. These are the principles I have shared in this text.

God is my ultimate source of inspiration. About a decade ago, I began to make radical changes in my life; they began with my thinking about God. I see this world in very black and white terms, and it helps me make a little sense of its complexity.

I made a decision to view life and all I see in it from one of two perspectives. The first perspective is that *everything comes from nothing*. The second is *everything comes from Everything*. This is a very broad idea that has led me to more and more searching, but it gave me a starting point for my search.

It is probably no surprise that I have chosen the latter view; everything comes from Everything. This choice helped me begin evolving as a leader.

No matter where you are on your journey, my hope is that this book can help you along the way. And it is my belief that all of us were made for something great, something so much greater than ourselves.

My desire for this book is to provide a resource for the story you are writing….and make no mistake, we are all writing a story.

Here is to your Evolution As A Leader!

Suggested Reading and Resources

Books

- The Holy Bible

Listed in alphabetical order by author

- Tape Breakers, Maximize Your Impact with People You Love, Teams You Lead, and Causes that Stir Your Heart, Jim Akers

- Servant Leadership In Action: How You Can Achieve Great Relationships and Results, Ken Blanchard & Renee Broadwell

- Dare to Lead: Brave Work, Tough Conversations, Whole Hearts, Brené Brown, Ph.D.

- Daring Greatly: How the Courage to Be Vulnerable Transforms the Way We Live, Love, Parent, and Lead, Brené Brown, Ph.D.

- How to Win Friends & Influence People, Dale Carnegie

- Influence: The Psychology of Persuasion, Robert B. Cialdini, Ph.D.

- Integrity: The Courage to Meet the Demands of Reality, Dr. Henry Cloud

- The Power of The Other: The startling effect other people have on you, from the boardroom to the bedroom and beyond and what to do about it, Dr. Henry Cloud

- Good To Great: Why Some Companies Make The Leap...And Others Don't, Jim Collins

- The 7 Habits of Highly Effective People, Stephen Covey

- Little Black Book of Leadership: Essential Leadership Advice for New Managers, Todd Dewett Ph.D.

- Show Your Ink: Stories About Leadership and Life, Todd Dewett PH.D.

- The Effective Executive: The Definitive Guide to Getting the Right Things Done, Peter F. Drucker

- Grit: The Power of Passion and Perseverance, Angela Duckworth

- Mindset: The New Psychology of Success, Carol S. Dweck, Ph.D.

- Tools of Titans: The Tactics, Routines, and Habits of Billionaires, Icons, and World-Class Performers, Timothy Ferris

- Tribe of Mentors: Short Life Advice from the Best in the World, Timothy Ferris

- Man's Search For Meaning, Viktor E. Frankl

- Give And Take: Why Helping Others Drives Our Success, Adam Grant, Ph.D.

- The Wisdom of Andrew Carnegie as Told to Napoleon Hill, Napoleon Hill

- Think & Grow Rich, Napoleon Hill

- The Servant: A Simple Story About the True Essence of Leadership, James C. Hunter

- Benjamin Franklin: An American Life, Walter Isaacson

- The One Thing, The Surprisingly Simple Truth Behind Extraordinary Results, Garry Keller and Jay Papasan

- The Inevitable: Understanding the 12 Technological Forces That Will Shape Our Future, Kevin Kelly

- The Five Dysfunctions of A Team: A Leadership Fable, Patrick Lencioni & Gary Noon

- The Power of Full Engagement: Managing Energy, Not Time, is the Key to High Performance and Personal Renewal, Jim Loehr and Tony Schwartz

- Be A People Person: Effective Leadership Through Effective Relationships, John C. Maxwell

- Developing the Leader Within You, John C. Maxwell

- Today Matters: 12 Daily Practices to Guarantee Tomorrow's Success, John C. Maxwell

- Leaders, Myth and Reality, General Stanley McChrystal, Jeff Eggers and Jason Mangone

- Andrew Carnegie, David Nasaw

- Seven Men: And the Secret of Their Greatness, Eric Metaxas

- Three Big Questions That Everyone Asks Sooner or Later, Dave Phillips

- Lincoln on Leadership: Executive Strategies for Tough Times, Donald T. Phillips

- Spiritual Leadership: Principles of Excellence For Every Believer, J. Oswald Sanders

- Leaders Eat Last, Why Some Teams Pull Together And Others Don't, Simon Sinek

- Leading With Integrity: Competence With Christian Character, Fred Smith Sr.& David L. Goetz

- The Next Generation Leader: Five Essentials for Those Who Will Shape the Future, Andy Stanley

- The Purpose Driven Life: What on Earth Am I Here For?, Rick Warren

On-Line Resources

- VEL INSTITUTE https://www.velinstitute.org/

- The Tim Ferriss Podcast https://tim.blog/podcast/

- The Learning Leader Podcast https://learningleader.com/the-podcast/

- Heart for Excellence Podcast
  http://heartforexcellence.com/

- EverSan Cooper Podcast
  https://www.eversancooper.com/podcast

Acknowledgements

[1] Michael Jordan, NBA.com
https://www.nba.com/history/legends/profiles/michael-jordan
[2] Anais Nin blog Herdacity, https://herdacity.org/anais-nin/
[3] Roosevelt, The Theodore Roosevelt Center, Dickinson State
University, https://www.theodorerooseveltcenter.org/
[4] Ancient Chinese Proverb
[5] The Power of the Other, Dr. Henry Cloud, Harper Business, 2016
[6] "Becoming Yourself: A conversation with Anna Quindlen, St. Louis
Magazine, Jeannette Cooperman, May 8, 2017
https://www.stlmag.com/culture/Literature/becoming-yourself-a-
conversation-with-anna-quindlen/
[7] Steven Pressfield, The Art of War: Break Through the Blocks and Win
Your Inner Creative Battles, Black Irish Entertainment, LLC, First Edition,
2012
[8] "Feel like a fraud," American Psychological Association, gradPSYCH
Magazine, Kirsten Weir, November 2013.
https://www.apa.org/gradpsych/2013/11/fraud
[9] Weir, Ibid
[10] Viktor E. Frankl, Man's Search for Meaning, Beacon Press, Fifth Ed.
2006.
[11] Frankl, Ibid
[12] Andy Stanley, Next Generation Leader, Five essentials for those who
will shape the future, Multnomah Books, 2003.
[13] Fredrik Haren – 2017 Global Leadership Summit, Aug. 10-11, 2017,
Live Simulcast. The Woodlands Church, The Woodlands TX
[14] Jenny Medeiros, Elon Musk: The Story of the Boy Who Changed the
Future, Goalcast, December 20, 2017
https://www.goalcast.com/2017/12/20/elon-musk-life-story/
[15] Henry Ford, Reader's Digest, September, 1947.
[16] Reader's Digest, Ibid
[17] James P. Carse, Finite and Infinite Games, A Vision of Life as Play
and Possibility. Free Press, 1986
[18] Peter Drucker, Goodreads.com, January 24, 2016
[19] John F. Kennedy Moon Speech, NASA, September 12, 1962.
https://er.jsc.nasa.gov/seh/ricetalk.htm
[20] "One Small Step for Man: Was Neil Armstrong Misquoted?",
Space.com, https://www.space.com/17307-neil-armstrong-one-small-
step-quote.html
[21] Franklin Quote - https://www.goodreads.com/quotes/1270715-an-
investment-in-knowledge-pays-the-best-interest
[22] Lumberjack story - Steven R. Covey, The & Habits of Highly Effective
People, Powerful Lessons in Personal Change, Simon &. Schuster, 25th
Anniversary Edition, 2004.
[23] Covey, Ibid

[24] Stephen King On Writing, A Memoir of the Craft, Scribner, 2000
[25] Pressfield, Ibid
[26] Covey, Ibid
[27] Bob Koenig, Founder of Andrew Coaching, www.andrewcoaching.com
[28] Andy Stanley, "2017 Global Leadership Summit"
[29] Goethe, quoted by Stephen Covey, Ibid.
[30] Frosty Westering, azquotes.com/quote/748466
[31] Carol S. Dweck, Ph.D., Mindset, The New Psychology of Success, Ballantine Books, 2016
[32] "exponential," Merriam-Webster, 2019, retrieved April 25th, 2019, from https://www.merriam-webster.com/dictionary/exponential
[33] Tim Ferriss, Tribe of Mentors, Houghton Mifflin Harcourt Publishing Company, 2017.
[34] Leadership Lessons from Gen. James Mattis (Ret.) https://youtu.be/3EYU3VTI3IU
[35] Matt Deggs, Judge Wayne Mack's 2018 Prayer Breakfast, Lone Star Convention Center.
[36] Andy Stanley, Ibid
[37] Jim Collins, Good to Great, HarperCollins Publishers, 2001.
[38] William James, https://www.goodreads.com/quotes/23215
[39] Andy Stanley, Ibid
[40] Joe R. Campa Jr. MCPON Addresses Deckplate Leadership at San Diego Conference, 3-1-2007 https://www.navy.mil/submit/display.asp?story_id=28073
[41]Bob Kapp, friend and mentor to many.
[42] David Nasaw, Andrew Carnegie, Penguin Books 2006.Summarized
[43] Andrew Carnegie, The Gospel of Wealth, The North American Review 1889
[44] Carnegie quoted from John C. Maxwell, The Maxwell Daily Reader, Thomas Nelson, Inc. 2007
[45] Napoleon Hill, The Wisdom of Andrew Carnegie, The Napoleon Hill Foundation, revised edition 2004
[46] Carnegie cited by Napoleon Hill Ibid p126
[47] Eric Metaxas, Seven Men and the Secret of their Greatness, Thomas Nelson, 2015 Summarized
[48] Abraham Lincoln Online.org http://www.abrahamlincolnonline.org
[49] Eric Metaxas, Seven Men Ibid. Lincoln summarized
[50] Eric Metaxas, Seven Men Ibid Washington summarized
[51] Abraham Lincoln Online.org http://www.abrahamlincolnonline.org
[52] Eric Metaxas, Seven Men. Ibid Washington
[53] Murray, Goodreads - https://www.goodreads.com/quotes/67769-until-one-is-committed-there-is-hesitancy-the-chance-to
[54] Todd Dewett and Terry Weaver, VEL INSTITUTE Podcast,

https://www.velinstitute.org/todd-dewett/
[55] Dewett &Weaver Ibid
[56] General Stanley McChrystal, World Affairs of Greater Houston - talk about Leaders: Myth and Reality, Dec. 4th, 2018.
[57] Leo Tolstoy, Three Methods of Reform (1900)
[58] James C. Hunter, The Servant, A Simple Story About the True Essence of Leadership, Crown Business Books, 2012
[59] M.H.McKee, Rancher & Author
http://greatthoughtstreasury.com/author/m-h-mckee
[60] Dr. Henry Cloud, Integrity, the courage to meet the demands of reality, Harper, 2006.
[61] Stanley McChrystal, Jeff Eggers and Jason Mangone, Leaders Myth and Reality, Portfolio / Penguin, 2018 – Disney Summarized.
[62] Leaders, Myth and Reality, Ibid
[63] Leaders, Myth and Reality, Ibid
[64] Disney on Youtube….
https://www.youtube.com/watch?time_continue=20&v=8rujLwY1C8k
[65] Dale Carnegie, How to Win Friends & Influence People, Pocket Books, Revised Edition 1981. Lincoln Summarized
[66] Tim Ferriss, Tribe of Mentors, Houghton Mifflin Harcourt Publishing, 2017, Eleanor Roosevelt,
[67] Covey, Ibid
[68] The Dalai Lama, The Path to Tranquility, DAILY WISDOM HIS HOLINESS THE DALAI LAMA, Viking / Arkana Penguin Group, 1998.
[69] Ralph Waldo Emerson, Worship, https://emersoncentral.com/texts/the-conduct-of-life/worship/
[70] Covey, Ibid
[71] Leaders: Myth and Reality Ibid
[72] Servant Leadership in Action, Edited by Ken Blanchard & Rene Broadwell, Barrett-Koehler Publishers Inc. 2018
[73] Servant Leadership in Action Ibid
[74] Robert Reiss interviews Simon Cooper, Forbes.com: How Ritz-Carlton Stays At The Top, Oct. 30, 2009
[75] Forbes: How Ritz-Carlton Stays At The Top, Ibid
[76] John C. Maxwell, quoting David Hartley-Leonard, Developing the Leader Within You, Thomas Nelson 1993.
[77] Bob Koenig permission given
[78] Tape Breakers, Jim Akers, Copyright Jim Akers, 2015, Disraeli Summarized
[79] Akers, Ibid
[80] Junno Arocho Esteves, Catholic News Service, Catholicnews.com 4/13/17
[81] Nobel Prize.org
https://www.nobelprize.org/prizes/peace/1952/schweitzer/biographical/
Schweitzer Summarized

[82] Schweitzer Quote https://www.forbes.com/quotes/222/
[83] Pat Tillman Foundation https://pattillmanfoundation.org/ Tillman Summarized
[84] Pat Tillman a Football Life, Arizona Cardinals, Video https://www.azcardinals.com/video/pat-tillman-a-football-life-18006935
[85] Steve McKinney, 2018 VEL INSTITUTE Legacy Awards Speech, Nov. 10th 2018.
[86] James Allen, As A Man Thinketh, Peter Pauper Press, 1960
[87] Lao Tzu
[88] Emma Wenner, Publishersweekly.com, July Religion Bestsellers, Aug 09, 2017.
[89] Rick Warren, Purpose Driven Life, What On Earth Am I Here For? Zondervan, 2002.
[90] Socrates quoted by Dave Phillips in Three Big Questions, Copyright 2015 by Dave Phillips.
[91] Louis Carroll quoted by Dave Phillips in Three Big Questions, Copyright 2015 by Dave Phillips.
[92] Phillips, Three Big Questions, Ibid
[93] Quote Investigator https://quoteinvestigator.com/2016/06/22/why/
[94] Adam Smith, Comparison is the Death of Joy, Asmithblog.com, Oct. 8, 2017.
[95] Jim Bishop, The Golden Ham: A Candid Biography of Jackie Gleason, Simon and Schuster, 1956.
[96] Goodreads Quotes https://www.goodreads.com/quotes/473110-it-is-perfectly-true-as-philosophers-say-that-life-must
[97] David Booth and Masayuki Machiya, The Arts Go to School, Stenhouse Publishers, 2004
[98] The Caged Bird Legacy, Celebrating 90 Years https://www.mayaangelou.com/2018/04/26/celebrate-90-years/
[99] PBS-TV, American Masters, "Maya Angelou." http://www.pbs.org/wnet/americanmasters/maya-angelou-film/7533/
[100] Maya Angelou, I Know Why the Caged Bird Sings, Random House 2015
[101] Ibid
[102] Ibid
[103] Oprah Winfrey, Oprah Talks to Maya Angelou, The Oprah Magazine, December 2000
[104] Tyler Perry, Live Kelly and Ryan, October 20, 2018. https://www.youtube.com/watch?v=jSaJJdHeXrw
[105] J. Oswald Sanders, Spiritual Leadership, Moody Publishers, 2007
[106] McChrystal speech, Ibid
[107] Stephen Covey, Living the 7 Habits: Stories of Courage and Inspiration, Free Press, 2000, Page 47

[108] Daniel Wiser Jr. Lincoln's Faith, April 14, 2017, National Review
https://www.nationalreview.com/2017/04/abraham-lincoln-religion/
[109] President Ronald Reagan, Aug. 23rd, 1984 Prayer Breakfast
https://www.reaganfoundation.org/ronald-reagan/reagan-quotes-speeches/remarks-at-an-ecumenical-prayer-breakfast-in-dallas-texas/
[110] John Wooden, UCLA Newsroom, June 4, 2010
http://newsroom.ucla.edu/releases/xx-wooden-seven-point-creed-84181
[111] Warren, Bertrand Russell, quoted in Purpose Driven Life, Ibid
[112] Philosoblog,com, Pablo Picasso,
https://philosiblog.com/2014/07/02/inspiration-exists-but-it-has-to-find-you-working/
[113] Pressfield, The War of Art, Ibid
[114] Albert Einstein https://www.goodreads.com/quotes/6882601-those-who-have-the-privilege-to-know-have-the-duty
[115] Russian Proverb, Gary Keller with Jay Papasan, The One Thing, The Surprisingly Simple Truth Behind Extraordinary Results, Bard Press, 2013
[116] Stanley quoting Hendricks, Next Generation Leader, Ibid
[117] Peter Drucker, The Effective Executive, Harper Business 2006
[118] Andrew Carnegie, Student Address, Curry Commercial College of Pittsburg, Pennsylvania June 23, 1885.
[119] How to Win Friends and Influence People, Ibid, Charles Schwab Summarized
[120] William Gaddis, The Recognitions, Dalkey Archive Press, 1983
[121] The Ritz-Carlton, Gold Standards,
http://www.ritzcarlton.com/en/about/gold-standards
[122] Robert Reiss interviews Simon Cooper, Forbes.com: How Ritz-Carlton Stays At The Top, Oct. 30, 2009
[123] Keller and Papasan, The One Thing Ibid
[124] Stephen Covey, The 7 Habits Ibid
[125] Stanley, Next Generation Leader, Ibid
[126] Aesop's Fables, The Goose That Laid the Golden Eggs
[127] James C. Collins and Jerry I. Porras, Built To Last, Successful Habits of Visionary Companies, HarperBusiness, 2002
[128] Chambers, Spiritual Leadership, Ibid
[129] Bob Koenig, Ibid
[130] Stanley, Next Generation Leader, Ibid
[131] Carnegie, How to Win Friends and Influence People, Ibid
[132] Dr. Mark Haywood, Professor of Preaching and Teaching for Impact, Grace School of Theology, 2018
[133] Stanley, Next Generation Leader, Ibid
[134] Zig Ziglar, Sources of Insight http://sourcesofinsight.com/zig-ziglar-quotes/
[135] Kevin Kelly, The Inevitable, Understanding the 12 Technological Forces That Will Shat Our Future, Viking, 2016

[136] Newton's 1st Law of Motion

[137] John Maxwell, Live To Lead Conference 2018, re-broadcasted by Barry Blanton and Chad Patterson

[138] Abraham Lincoln, https://www.azquotes.com/quote/611935

[139] Steve McKinney, VEL INSTITUTE Podcast, https://www.velinstitute.org/steve-mckinney/ Oct. 12th, 2018.

[140] McKinney Ibid, was quoting Henry Ford.

[141] Dr. Todd Dewett, is the author of "Show Your Ink," Ink Magazine Top 100 Leadership Speaker, on Jan. 21, 2016 at a VEL Keynote in The Woodlands Texas.

[142] Brené Brown, "Dare to Lead", Random House, 2018

[143] Brené ibid page 11

[144] Bronnie Ware, Blog, "Regrets of the Dying." https://bronnieware.com/blog/regrets-of-the-dying/

[145] VEL INSTITUTE Podcast https://www.velinstitute.org/general-hummer/ Recorded July 6th, 2018

[146] Angela Duckworth, Grit, The Power of Passion and Perseverance, Scribner, 2016. Summarized

[147] Will Smith, NBC Today Show, Hancock Interview Jun. 23, 2008.

[148] Will Smith, Charlie Rose Interview, Mar. 13, 2002.

[149] Rose Interview, Ibid

[150] Will Smith, Steve Kroft Interview, 60 Minutes, Dec. 2, 2007

[151] Will Smith, Travis Smiley Interview

[152] Will Smith, Discipline Your Mind, http://www.whateverittakesmotivation.com/2018/03/02/discipline-mind-will-smith-full-speech/

[153] The Tim Ferriss Show: LeBron James and Mike Macias (#349) Nov. 27, 2018

[154] Dwayne Johnson The Greatest Speech Ever, Mulligan Brothers, Jun. 7, 2018. https://www.youtube.com/watch?v=ES4GBLTmQn8

[155] Dwayne Johnson https://en.wikipedia.org/wiki/Dwayne_Johnson , Summarized

[156] David Goggins, Can't Hurt Me, Master Your Mind and Defy the Odds, Lioncrest Publishing, 2018.

[157] Nasaw, Andrew Carnegie, Ibid

[158] Bob Milner, Founder Terbo Consulting, Professor of Leadership and Entrepreneurship, Serial Entrepreneur.

[159] Collins, Good To Great, Ibid

[160] Collins, Good To Great, Ibid

[161] Collins, Good To Great, Ibid

[162] Collins, Good To Great, Ibid

[163] Johann Wolfgang von Goethe, https://www.goodreads.com/quotes/2326-things-which-matter-most-

must-never-be-at-the-mercy

[164] Alice Schroder, The Snowball, Bantam Books, 2009

[165] Duckworth, Grit, Ibid

[166] Covey, Seven Habits, Ibid

[167] "This is billionaire Jeff Bezos' daily routine and it sets him up for success," by Ali Montag, CNBC "Make it," September 15, 2018. https://www.cnbc.com/2018/09/14/billionaire-jeff-bezos-shares-the-daily-routine-he-uses-to-succeed.html

[168] Montag, CNBC, Ibid

[169] Franklin, Benjamin, The Autobiography of Benjamin Franklin, Eds. Stanley Appelbaum and Philip Smith, Dover Publications, Inc. 1996

[170] Akers, Tape Breakers, Ibid

[171] Franklin D. Roosevelt, Inaugural Address, March 4th, 1933 https://www.archives.gov/education/lessons/fdr-inaugural

[172] Proverbs 4:23 (NIV)

[173] Neale Donald Walsch, blog, "Life Begins at the end of your comfort zone." https://1440.org/blog/life-begins-at-the-end-of-your-comfort-zone-talking-with-neale-donald-walsch/

[174] The long short trader, Michael Jordan's Hall of Fame Enshrinement Speech – highly applicable to market participants. https://thelongshorttrader.com/2013/02/18/michael-jordans-hall-of-fame-enshrinement-speech-highly-applicable-to-market-participants/

[175] Margaret Meade, 1982 March 3, 100 Mile House Free Press, Planetary Initiative group forms, Quote Page 16, Column 1, 100 Mile House, British Columbia, Canada.

[176] Perry, ibid Nov. 2nd, 2018

[177] Akers, quoting Albert Einstein in Tape Breakers, Ibid

[178] Bob Koenig adapted from Donald Rumsfeld, There are known knowns, https://en.wikipedia.org/wiki/There_are_known_knowns

[179] Leaders, Myth and Reality, Ibid.

[180] Eleanor Roosevelt, 1987 October 28, The Hutchinson News, Hutchinson, Kansas. (NewsBank Access World News)

[181] Oliver Wendell Holmes, https://www.risebeyond.org/10-quotes-on-collaboration/

[182] Grant Freeland, Talent Wins Games, Teamwork Wins Championships, Forbes.com Jun 1, 2018.

[183] Jordan Hall of Fame speech, Naismith Memorial Basketball Hall of Fame 2009 https://www.youtube.com/watch?v=XLzBMGXfK4c

[184] Michael Jordan, NBA Advanced Stats, https://stats.nba.com/player/893/career/

[185] Stanley, Ibid

About the Author

Terry Weaver enlisted in the U.S. Navy in 1999 as a Navy Corpsman. He was deployed as a combat medic with the U.S. Marines and served a tour of duty in Iraq in 2002 and 2003. After five years of active duty, Terry received an honorable discharge.

He attended Mays Business School at Texas A&M and received the Tillman Military Scholarship from the namesake foundation of Army Ranger and NFL star player Pat Tillman. Terry earned a Bachelor of Business Administration.

He then spent ten years in corporate America in the heavy transportation sales and marketing industry.

In 2014, Terry co-founded VEL Institute a 501 (c) (3) nonprofit with a mission to "Develop Veterans, Entrepreneurs, and Leaders in a collaborative and educational environment so that they will have a greater impact in their families, organizations, and communities."

In 2015, Terry was hired as an Associate Pastor at the Ark Church and served as pastor for two years. In 2018, Terry stepped out in faith to move into a full-time role as the Executive Director of VEL Institute. He is currently working on his Masters of Biblical Studies at Grace School of Theology.

In 2019 Terry joined the founding board of the Tillman Academy, a K – 12 charter school, being founded in the namesake of Pat Tillman to serve needed areas of Montgomery County. Tillman Academy will teach the importance of civil duty, leadership, and character to the next generation of leaders.

Terry was also selected as a leading actor in the forthcoming eight-episode TV series, Breaking Strongholds which is being filmed and produced in Montgomery, Texas.

Terry is happily married with four children. He is passionate about studying leadership and believes that the greatest act of leadership is leading someone toward Christ.

To learn more about VEL Institute please visit: www.velinstitute.org

58980550R00152

Made in the USA
Columbia, SC
29 May 2019